Love & Gratitude

by

Natasha Dao

I0148513

First published in Australia 2013 by

Natasha Dao, Brisbane

natashadao@lovinggratitude.com

www.lovinggratitude.com

Copyright © 2013 Natasha Dao

All rights reserved. This publication may not be reproduced, stored in a retrieval system or transmitted, in any form or by any means, electronic, mechanical, photocopying, recording or otherwise, without the prior written permission of the publishers and copyright holders.

National Library of Australia Cataloguing-in-Publication entry

Love & Gratitude:

Empower, transform... a new guide to living your life with a higher purpose

ISBN: 978-0-9923807-1-7

Subjects: Self-actualization (Psychology)
Self-realization
Love
Gratitude

155.2

Primary Editor: Amanda Morgan

Editor: Nyrie Roos

Cover Photography: Phi-Hung Le-Vu

Printed in America by Lulu Press, Inc.

Being Grateful is a sheer measure of honouring
your inner Love to be able to see it in
others Kindness of Love in return.

Appreciate and feel blessed of life's
every given moment to experience fully with
Love, Gratitude, enthusiasm and inner Happiness.

LOVE & GRATITUDE

Empower, transform... a new guide to living your life with a higher purpose

Dedication

My deepest Love & Gratitude goes to my Grandmother, who to me is a very strong and inspirational female figure in my family. Because of her admirable strength and courage in standing alone by her seven children as they migrated to Australia after the Vietnam War. Today, my family and I are very fortunate enough to have the opportunity to create a better future and state of living. I am very blessed for having such a wonderful loving and influential Grandmother. She has made a profound impact on me, and I give thanks for everything I am experiencing along this journey called life.

Table of Contents

Preface

This book has been written in appreciation of the empowered, confident and happy person that I have become today, living the dream of my life as an author and entrepreneurial philanthropist, but remembering my humble beginnings. Whoo Hoo! I am loving and embracing every moment of the excitement and adventure of continual self-growth and learning as a liberated and modern woman, and of what I stand for as who I AM. I am creating a fulfilling journey for my life, travelling in the right direction towards meeting my bigger goals and dreams. This is the start of my journey into discovering my higher purpose in life.

Once in every human lifetime, at some stage or another, there will be a point where our lives may come to a cross-road in the quest to restate and redefine our sense of ourselves within the whole scope of the meaning of life, the so-called moment of awakening or epiphany to our higher purpose. So what is your heart's life purpose? Are you living a fulfilled and happy life?

These are some of the many questions I asked myself in moments of awakening as I travelled along the path to seeing and understanding what was really of importance — my role and purpose on this earth — all while I went through university and in my career years, more than 10 years ago. But after many turbulent times, and dealing with years of traumatising abuse, I have countered the effects of my ordeal to seek and find the true higher purpose of my life and self. There were great challenges in the life lessons and wisdom I have learned about my now much loved, improved and empowered self — the ability to recognise truth from deep within the heart and soul, to succumb to a state of awareness of Love & Gratitude in all of my hardships, trials and tribulations, and life experiences.

This has lead me to give birth to my first significant book, with the purpose of bringing forth a message to help others, to also empower and transform their lives through the healing that comes from activating their inner Love & Gratitude and applying it to all aspects of life, to find their higher purpose and life-awakening calling — the real meaning and purpose to life.

I believe everyone is here on earth to serve a profound purpose and to give to others. That is why I am giving back by sharing my teaching stories and wisdom, to help you take positive steps towards empowering yourself to live the life that you deserve, and awaken to the true path to your goals and dreams. You know you are capable of anything in life when you set your mind intentionally and with an open heart to a genuine purpose or goal.

Create a better world by living with the purpose of sharing a fulfilling life with love and gratitude. I am grateful that I can share my life lessons and experiences with you, and I pray that my guidance and the steps I teach will help you achieve a new level of self-empowerment and bring abundance and happiness for you to live a more fulfilled of a higher purpose life; thus, fostering a world conscious of love, peace, unity and harmony for all humankind.

Acknowledgements

I would like to honour and thank the people who collaborated and contributed towards helping me make my first book possible, Amanda Morgan; Nyrie Roos; Publishing Catapult; Phi-Hung Le-Vu; Greg Gahan. Plus, there were many others who have been part of my life experiences and who have helped and taught me to become a much wiser and a more empowered self within Love & Gratitude, so that I have graciously found my path to my higher purpose of life.

My humble of Love & Gratitude to you all!

Introduction

In the circle of life, we as humans are born to learn, grow, inspire and thrive as unique individuals and collectively, as a whole universe of magnificent beings, empowered with confidence to take strides into new dimensions, to move beyond mediocrity and live a more fulfilled and happy life. By stepping out of our comfort zone to genuinely seek out greater gifts to give and serve others, to use the blessings we have been given, for the empowerment of ourselves and others. Our journey is to discover and embrace a higher purpose of life. This can only be achieved through healing and activating our inner Love & Gratitude in every aspect of life. Now is the right time to empower and transform yourself to live the life that you deserve, in awakening to the right path to your goals and dreams.

Start living your life by opening your heart and your mind to a multitude of possibilities. By opening your heart to a new level of abundance with gratitude for love, life and happiness, you can achieve anything that you set your mind to. All it will take is an honest desire to love, a passion for life and the pursuit of happiness in everything you do. When you love the world around you, the world will love you in return. When you care about life, then life will care for you. When you search for happiness, you will realise that you had it all along.

The desire for happiness lies within you, and who and what you draw into your life creates and expands that happiness around you. An old adage says to start off by being humble, happy and comfortable with loving yourself first and foremost, and love and happiness will be received in return. Also, a positive outlook on life empowers your yourself and overall life. You create your life outcomes by the effort you put into your cause, and the effects which consequently reflect your choices and the decisions you make. To look at it another way, you are in control of your destiny and in your life are always choices to be made, as long as you have self-knowledge and are aware and take responsibility for those choices.

Life's greatest treasures can be found within the people that you interact with every day and the circumstances that you create. When you get involved in life by attending special gratitude moments, making new friends and reaching out to the people around you, you will see the natural beauty that is in our world. The more that you are willing to experience life with an open heart, the happier you will eventually be.

It may sound simple and idealistic, but I have witnessed this working again and again. Life is really what you make of it, and the possibilities are endless when you have the right attitude and mindset. This book will take you through 27 inspiring and life-changing steps to help find your higher self and your true calling in this life through the healing and empowerment of personal growth and development. It will help you to activate your inner love and gratitude and apply them to all aspects of life. Within the spiritual realm, you will have healing, and discover a sense of inner peace, self-love, freedom and all the abundance of life and happiness, so you can love the life that you deserve and find the right path for your life's journey of fulfilment, by claiming a new and improved self.

2

I hope this book inspires the best that lies within you, and helps you transform your life, to find the power to make an impact on your own life and that of others — all by activation of the inner love and gratitude you apply in every aspect of your life. Create a better world by living with the purpose of sharing a fulfilling life with love and gratitude. I am grateful that I can share my life lessons and experiences with you, and I pray that my guidance and the steps I teach will help you achieve a new level of self-empowerment and bring abundance and happiness for you to live a more fulfilled higher purpose life.

1. Giving & Sharing Love!

Happiness starts when you find a way to love yourself and then choose to share that love with the rest of the world. Love has no real power if you keep it hidden inside. Giving and sharing your love and your gratitude for the world around you is vital in finding happiness within your life. By being able to physically, mentally and emotionally connect with other people, you will feel an abundance of personal and spiritual rewards.

Two of the easiest ways for you to give and share your love are through verbal and physical exchanges of affection. No, I am not referring to sexual relations, but the even more powerful, emotional loving gestures of compassion and concern. Just by giving a real and meaningful kiss, a gesture of kind words in caring acknowledgement for another, a warm hug or even by holding another person's hand, you are giving and sharing your love.

Loving gestures that you share with others need not to be always intimate in any way, but simply in any meaningful form of kindness or action (e.g. by giving someone a flower or a friendly embrace when you see they are in need of some cheering up). Showing how much you care and love them through these kind of actions, brings an immense appreciation and understanding for one another and the joy of sharing your love.

Your intention of giving your love and sharing it with another must be from the heart and driven by love and compassion. This usually can be seen in what we express in our actions and the kindness we show. You should not expect any reciprocal love in return for what you give. However, it is nice to be loved and to have your loving actions acknowledged and appreciated by others. We all love to be loved openly and freely and to give to, and share with those we care deeply for in our lives. Innately, this is what we know best — giving and sharing as loving and compassionate souls — it is our natural birthright as humans to do so.

> *Wherever Love is expressed and shared amongst one another, there will always be bountiful of Love in return in continuous full circle which flowers the breath called life.* — *Natasha Dao*

Doesn't it feel fantastic to just squeeze somebody special and feel the warmth of their arms around you?

You know the kind of embrace that I mean. It is that intimate moment when you are giving someone more than just a friendly hug. It becomes a powerful connection that can soothe us when we are angry, calm us when we are upset, or lift our spirits when we are feeling sad. It is one of the most natural and comforting ways we physically show love for someone else.

Being in contact with another person physically, in the embrace of each other's arms, allows us to bond and connect on a compassionate, personal level, and it is healthy to display of such loving affection. Generally, I love hugs, especially when I am sharing that hug with someone special who feels deeply the mutual and respectful love between us. I know that when I share my hugs with others, I feel incredibly at ease, comforting and lovingly warm and happy inside. This probably explains why I enjoy giving and receiving hugs so much.

Embracing another is an amazing and wonderful feeling — to show how much you love and appreciate the other person in your life and vice versa. Everyone loves to feel loved with the warmth of another's arms embrace and touch. The sense of 'hominess' love and security is what we are designed as human beings to desire. Do you ever wonder why newborn babies are tightly and snugly wrapped in their blankets by the nurses after they have just been birthed into the world?

Studies have shown that in our purest young birth life forms, we instinctively feel vulnerable. The sense of warmth and safety while developing and growing in our mother's womb for 9 months keeps us feeling very loved and secure. So, in order to create and maintain the same feeling of loving embrace, babies are treated in this manner. The same goes for adults; we too need this sort of embrace from time to time, to feel loved, cherished and appreciated. All by means of a loving embrace or hug! There is nothing wrong in demonstrating this kind of loving embrace to whomever you wish, at any given time or place, as long it feels natural to do so. Get out there and give someone a hug today!

> *Love gives vibrancy to life, the manifold reasons for life to live and thrive.*
> *— Natasha Dao*

2. Express and Share Your Love, Starting with the Family

Why don't we greet everyone with a big warm embrace?

Could you imagine walking into a restaurant and hugging the hostess?

We might not be able to hug everyone that we see, and nor should we, but the world would be a much kinder and more friendly place if we could. However, as a society we DO need to *physically* show our love for each other often, especially to the people who are closest to us. We should keep this in mind, starting with our family, because the family is the deep core of our love and affection in relationships and the foundation for developing a healthy, nurturing love of family and the self.

> *I think today the world is upside down, and is suffering so much because there is so very little love in the home, and in family life. We have no time for our children, we have no time for each other, there is no time to enjoy each other. Love begins at home; love lives in homes, and that is why there is so much suffering and so much unhappiness in the world today.... Everybody today seems to be in such a terrible rush, anxious for greater developments and greater riches and so on, so that children have very little time for their parents. Parents have very little time for each other, and in the home begins the disruption of the peace of the world.*

— *Mother Teresa*, Loving Jesus (ed, Jose Luis Gonzalez-Balado), St. Anthony Messenger Press; 1991.

A loving and nurturing family background helps us to develop a feeling of shared love and support, and gain a deeper understanding of who we really are and what we become in later life. Unfortunately, not everyone is blessed with a loving family; in many cases, especially in many third world countries, individuals and children are belittled and don't know what a caring family is really like — the word 'love' is absent from their lives. They have no choice about the situation life has placed them in, in circumstances of conflict, corruption and poverty. This unfairness is due to a lack of love in their lives. People in these situations do not know and experience what love really entails.

It all starts in the home and within the family. So, be grateful that you are blessed with a family, regardless of whether it provides a little or a lot of love, because you can always invoke love by contributing loving actions and kind, caring words to your family members. Be connected, be respectful, be considerate and demonstrate your love, even by saying 'I love you dad! Or mum! Or sister! Or brother!'.

Love expressed within the family is crucial, especially in today's busy world with its many work commitments and the daily deluge of activity. We tend to forget the simple things in life and the necessity of being appreciative of one another, of expressing affection by sharing a loving embrace, an acknowledgement of caring about how your loved ones are feeling and your interest in their day. This is enough to build a close, loving and caring connection and an open exchange of communication.

A parent may have a dreadful day at work and then come home to be aggravated, upset or annoyed by their children or family. It is easy to show anger or cry, as an outlet for this, without knowing how to

express your feelings, except to lash out at anyone or anything that stands in your way. Stop the temptation to create uproar and escalate the situation with unpleasant behaviour. Otherwise, you will only create conflict, building on the anger, pain and hurtful words that are created in that moment.

You have probably experienced this in your own life or as an observer. I know I have, on numerous occasions with my family, loved ones and other relationships. I have to admit, it is definitely a great challenge and I have constructively embraced it through the course of many lessons learned over time, to construct a better understanding and communication skill set. When you apply this skill set correctly, you create an empowering tool that will help you develop further insight into how to respond to people's emotions and help them, rather than reacting to them. This is what I call 'activating your inner love' by communicating from your heart with understanding and compassion, and it is much more sensible and wise too!

By approaching from an understanding, loving and compassionate view and simply asking the parent or partner why they are feeling or behaving like that, you are helping them to know that you care enough to communicate from a loving and understanding perspective. By asking 'Why?', you allow them to reflect consciously on their own unintentionally hurtful actions or words, and their effect on their loved ones.

Essentially, helping others to speak or letting them vent about their day to you can be therapeutic for them and will ease their frustration. To be able to release their stress and tension in this manner is soothing and healing. All they really need is your loving attention and desire to hear what they have to say at the end of their day. So, lend your loving ears, whenever your loved ones require them! They will appreciate your time and desire to hear them out, a sign that you care for and love them.

I often see or hear of a child coming home from school feeling mopey and sad, which is not their normal behaviour. They may have issues or personal problems at school, and do not wish to discuss them with their parents or family members. Simply because most parents are engrossed in their own busy day, they often do not take the time to find out why their child is like this, they think that everything is okay and do not bother to express their concerns for the child and their well-being.

In most cases, I feel the emotional connection between parents and children has lost something — what it means to unify and bond by communicating with care and loving understanding. Especially as, from a parent, it only takes a little devoted attention and time given to learning to understand their child or children better by just showing their concerns for them. It does not take much time for parents just to ask concerned questions in an act of love and care, such as: 'How was your day at school?' 'Did you enjoy yourself?' 'What did you learn today in school?' Always take care to be engaged in your children's lives and activities, and also with their friends. If you show enough love and care for their well-being, and provide continuous loving support for them, essentially being in their life, you will build a strong bond between you (e.g. attend their football games, school fair or musical concerts and school athletics).

Your child will love and appreciate you for just being attentive, caring parents, and look to you for guidance in life; you will become a close friend and their role model — someone to look up to. By keeping an open, loving and understanding channel of communication, you will bind the growing connections between you as the parent and your child. Then the child will reciprocate and openly share and be honest with you, allowing you to be part of their childhood, teenage and, possibly, adulthood life. You need to keep in mind though, that you need always to appreciate and provide all your intentions as best that you can to be caring parents to unify the family with continuous loving, understanding bonds.

Now, wouldn't the world be a much more loving and kind place if we could only take a minute of our time to just be in the moment and focus on what is going on within our family? There should be no excuses such as, 'I don't have the time' or 'I am too busy'. We all make time to do something else that suits us, right? Just by getting involved and giving each other the time to listen and speak, communicating from an understanding and compassionate heart. We can be at more ease and peaceful when solving and discussing each other's solutions and, hence, in creating a more loving nurturing family connection. Be the peacemaker and not the troublemaker!

3. Demonstrate Your Love with a Compassionate Hug

It feels good to hug someone and it is even more powerful when you know that it is having the same wonderful impact on the person you are hugging. Why deny yourself that incredibly powerful feeling of giving someone a really solid embrace?

Here is a little experiment to help you understand the power of a good hug.

Next time you hug someone, try to hold on for a few extra seconds and see if they try to pull away from you. When you feel that naturally inspired moment where you start to break apart, pull the other person back in closer to you. I am sure they will be enjoying the experience just as much as you are and they won't want it to stop either. It may even start an entirely new hug that ends up lasting twice as long. It is one of the simplest, yet most effective ways to connect with another human being, yet we seem to do it less often as we get older.

Giving a hug to someone can be medicinal and therapeutic and give a sense of healing. For instance, when someone is angry with you and although both of you have discussed the issues but some of the tension still lingers. Do not hesitate to throw your arms around them (within the right time of course) to soothe their restless minds, showering them with your love in a hug. You will be pleasantly surprised at how simply providing a hug can make all the difference in easing them and the situation. This is another tool of how a hug can be a powerful healing mechanism when you know that someone really needs one. So do not underestimate what a hug can do for you and for others. The epitome of what love stands for is really in the action of hugs.

There is nothing wrong with being affectionate to the people who matter most in your life. Love is meant to be shared. I know sometimes that means you may have to endure a sloppy wet kiss from your great aunt or uncle, but what harm is it really causing? A little lipstick on your cheek won't actually hurt you and it will make your aunt or uncle feel more connected to you. If you are fortunate enough to have a family that wants to show their love, then do not deprive them of the opportunity. There is never enough love to go around for sharing with all your family and relatives. This is the best way to express your love and care for them unconditionally.

Don't worry if you have to accept a few sticky icky kisses every once in a while! There will be enough really good kisses over the course of your life to make up for it. You know what I mean when I say a really good kiss! I am talking about those long passionate kisses that leave you with tingles from your head down to the tips of your toes. Those are the kinds of kisses that our hearts never will forget!

Over the course of your long life, there will be first kisses that will give you goose bumps and make the hair on your arms stand up straight. There will be gentle kisses on baby's foreheads, kisses to celebrate special occasions and romantic kisses that you will remember for a lifetime. Regardless of the reason, they all hold their own special meaning and they should not be avoided due to embarrassment or insecurities.

4. Pucker Up and Kiss Someone Today!

Let LOVE lead the light and into opening people's heart to RECEIVE love and SHARE their love onto others. — *Natasha Dao*

The love you give does not have to be physically shown, it can be emotional or mental support, or even just a kind word. You can show your love with a thoughtful gesture or an offer to help someone out when they are feeling overwhelmed. Love is any expression that connects two people and is based on mutual concern and affection. By sharing your love with someone else, you are creating a bond that will stand the test of time.

Life is meant to be spent giving and sharing your love freely with the people who matter most to you. There is no greater joy than loving someone and feeling the same love in return. It can make you feel warm and fuzzy inside, it can inspire passionate works of art and poetry, bringing your full colours into creativity or it can simply brighten a rainy day.

There is nothing better than feeling that passionate love you have for another in a romantic relationship. Where, with every breath, every waking moment, every heartbeat you are thinking of that person when they are not there with you. And they are feeling the same. It is the joy given by two hearts united and beating as one. When you are in that situation, it is like sunshine with streaming rays of illuminating lights filling you inner soul with colour, joy and laughter. Every inch of your body draws a very close bond between yourself and your lover or partner, as it is undeniably a force of nature.

When you are deeply in love with your partner, you may feel completely at home and safe, especially in their arms. Everything that surrounds you and your partner is beautiful and vibrantly coloured. Where it is as though time stands still when you are both together, for nothing really matters anymore besides bathing in each other's appreciative presence, not taking each other for granted, but savouring the endearing and loving connections that you experience together.

All your stress or woes of life are magically obliterated to nothingness, any fears or doubts that once existed are removed. So, when you feel you are falling in love with the other person and vice-versa, don't be afraid to fall hard and allow your heart to open up, allowing love bloom fully, and be invigorated with the feeling of mind and soul being complete. Treasure your love with honour, devotion and appreciation for each other. When your heart and mind are open to embrace all that love can create, you essentially become more understanding, appreciative, respectful and patient in every situation.

You and your partner cannot help but to be embraced into each other's arms with constant loving and caring touch. Continually mirroring each other's body language whenever you are both in close contact. Happily to express your warmth and care-free of heartfelt emotions is only when we know best to just be comfortably in yourself or in your shoes. Letting all your guards down and inhibitions to show with dignity, is genuinely coming through of our vulnerability for the other one to see with humbleness pride.

All of your physical affection and intense feelings of love, combined with those of your partner can only expand to a higher vibration Whenever both of your love frequencies are joined. This, to me, and I am very grateful to have experienced it, is the greatest feeling one human can ever feel. It accentuates understanding of how to love, and sharing that love with a special someone. Or, one can say it is the effect of submitting to feelings of ever-lasting euphoric love, but not the infatuation of love.

To be infatuated with another is more of a desire for love to share with that person merely in the realm of physical attraction or of an obsession for another without the feeling being mutual. You only think these feelings are love but unfortunately, they are not. The infatuated lover may be too engrossed in their own thoughts and the desire to trigger strong feelings in the other person, only longing desperately and wanting to always be with that person. Such feelings as these, I have distinguished through experience and learning how to identify what makes a genuine and healthy love relationship rather than a fleeting one-directional love. A non-reciprocal and unappreciative relationship is not desirable.

Give and Take

The old cliché that you will get back whatever you give in life is actually true! If you give unconditional love to those around you, then you will receive unconditional love in return. If your emotions are genuine and you openly share them, your love will inspire the same emotion in others. The notion of give and take in general encourages good energies to expand and circulate equally. When you choose to give unconditionally in good faith, more good will is given to you in return. This is essentially a reflection of karma and an understanding of cause and effect.

A mutual exchange of love is the greatest bond two people can share with each other. Both people should care about each other and want to be there for one another without hesitation or reservation. It is the way love was meant to work, even though it is not always the way it ends up happening.

In every relationship, now and then both people will need to compromise to fulfil each other's needs and desires, in order to sustain a give and take loving relationship. If you really love and care for that person, then it should not be hard to do whatever it is to please the other and to make them happy, and vice versa. After all, a true, loving relationship is all about complete trust, respect and good communication, understanding and appreciation, which leads to the growth of duality in love.

When a person shows you their devotion and their undying love, they will take part in the constant changes and actions that allow a reciprocal loving, caring relationship to take shape. Your every expression and action will align to those of your partner and you will submit to the synchronicity of each other's footsteps. Leading, guiding, continuous learning and nurturing the love between the two of you, creates a bridge of deeper understanding and growth for a happy, enduring and loving life together.

In a loving reciprocal relationship, love should be boundless, affection displayed to one another unconditionally and with ease. Without any hesitation or embarrassment to mutually give love and affection, and show tender care for each other can only demonstrate the gratifying meaning of a true, loving connection between two intertwined and empowering energies.

> *Love with passion and also with a profusion of compassion, but not with guilt or despair. Freely give and take unconditionally and always with acceptance and a mind to love adventurously and spontaneously.*
> — *Natasha Dao*

If you are not feeling the same love in return, then maybe your love has been misplaced. Not everyone out there is willing to accept and return your love, so it is important that you know how to separate yourself when the relationship you are in is not balanced. A relationship should not be based on one person giving love and the other person only taking your love, without offering any support or compassion in return. It is a partnership, which means both parties need to be involved in both the giving and the taking.

> *Giving connects two people, the giver and the receiver, and this connection gives birth to a new sense of belonging.* — *Deepak Chopra*

Have you ever watched a close friend in a bad relationship?

It is so hard to watch someone who you care about being mistreated or neglected by someone else, especially when their kindness has been taken advantage of. Witnessing the grief and emotional pain they endure, is a terrible experience. The mistreatment, unfair actions and disrespect for the other person in verbal and non-verbal. It is necessary to speak loudly on behalf of third parties when you see them being treated selfishly; it is wrong and downright inappropriate and inhuman to treat another in such ways.

When you see this happen, do not hesitate to intervene with caring

21

actions to help and protect the one in need. Help to sort them out with your kindness of care by asking if they are ok and whether they need help? In many cases, people might be embarrassed, especially when the situation occurs in public and may not accept your helpful gesture. If you are a good friend and care enough about their well-being, you will take the initiative to talk through with them the problems they are facing. Even if they are reluctant to be open with you, just probe with caring questions, be patient and allow them to comfortably speak about their problems with you.

Provide advice on what they need to do to in order to seek outside professional help or counselling if required, but always be there to provide them with unconditional love and support, and be a shoulder to lean on when they are in need. It goes a long way when you, as a caring friend, give them your help in times that are tough. Give them your devoted attention and listen to their troubles. Your loving actions show care for them, and demonstrate a friend of great loyalty.

They will thank you for helping them to see that the relationship they were involved in was actually a stifling and toxic relationship. Opening their eyes to help them recognise they have the power to choose to take control of their life and empower themselves to make the decision to remove themselves from the unhealthy relationship, and recognise these are good reasons to move on with life. Everyone now and then needs a good friend to be there and support them when they are really in need of help. We all deserve to be respected and treated with respect and treat with own dignity. So please do the same for others.

Mistreating others with a lack of respect, is truly a reflection of mistreating and disrespecting yourself and demeaning what it means to love yourself. Be conscious of how you treat others next time, you may discover new learnings about yourself and how you are unaware of projecting them onto others.

Now, have you ever stayed in a bad relationship?

Be honest. The only person you have to answer to is yourself.

We have all at some point or another given everything we have to offer to another person and then received absolutely nothing in return. I am not referring to material gifts or anything with a financial value. The best gifts in life are free, and matter more than anything you can purchase at a store.

I am talking about giving your time, your love and support freely without any expectations and then having that person abandon you when you need them the most. A relationship that lacks unconditional love is selfish if the other person continually is the taker and does not give in return. It is even worse is when it happens with someone that you really care about and they do not even realise that their behaviour is unfair.

Have you ever willingly given all of yourself to someone who mattered to you and that other person continuously enjoyed your generosity and support without ever offering you a shoulder to lean on, even during those times when you needed it the most?

That is not a give and take relationship.

Loving someone who matters to you the most, and that you strongly care for, is very hard to deal with, knowing that person shows no interest and care of love for you. This is an unfortunate experience

23

and I have sadly gone through such relationships in the past. You feel that you have been taken for granted and not been acknowledged for your boundless love and devotion towards the other person. Your energy is continually and relentlessly drained by their insensitivity and lack of feeling, leaving you in an emotional and unhappy state. It is physically and emotionally draining to be in such a relationship, where you are blind to the truth of the other person constantly taking and not fondly reciprocating.

At times, you might be in denial, believing that person can change for the better or awaken to their unfair behaviour. You do all that you can, and try to effectively communicate with them by expressing your thoughts and feelings about the unfairness of the relationship; instead, that person continues to be reluctant to care about your concerns, and seems to see only one side of the issues through self-ignorance and their own view of the benefits.

Did you accept their poor treatment?

Or did you decide it was time to move on?

Whether it is a selfish friend, a spoiled lover or a greedy family member, we all become a victim to somebody else at some point in our life. We all have put up with that buddy who conveniently forgets his wallet at home or the friend who monopolises every conversation. We all know these inconsiderate people and we readily accept their behaviour.

Why?

There is nothing wrong with giving and not expecting to receive anything in return. It is quite noble and there should be more people who are willing to be so selfless. The important thing is to make sure that you know where to draw the line. Give your love to the ones that truly are deserving of your love. Love should be genuinely shared by two people, creating an abundance of laughter and happiness in a long-term exchange of respect and appreciation. Your love is a valuable gift, so try to give it wisely.

Everybody deserves to find the right person and be in a genuine life-long loving relationship that completes them and the other in full appreciation, trust and in give and take. The main key here is to be appreciative of one another's love and never be selfish by taking that love for granted. It is only through the many loving encounters in our life that we are able to find within ourselves how love should be shared equally and wholeheartedly in contentment.

If you feel you are deserving of that 'contentment love', then you are allowing yourself to open your heart to embrace a genuine loving relationship that speaks to each of your desires, and your intention to have a complete give and take relationship. Do not reserve your love when you see that you are not in the right loving relationship, as it all starts out from a loving and compromising bond between two people.

Many people in relationships have discounted their love in return, by selfishly stroking their own egos at the expense of the other person's love and taking it for granted. For instance, not valuing and appreciating another person shows a lack of valuing and appreciating of oneself. Seeing that your partner does not have the same level of love and feelings you have felt from the start of the relationship. This demonstrates the unfairness and selfishness of those who do not take others' feelings into account.

If we are seeking mutual love and growth, to acknowledge and respect each other, finding common ground will help us to bring about a sense of appreciation and expand our love and help us to grow together. Sometimes, by pushing each other's buttons or in helping to challenge one another, we are discovering how to understand and learn more about ourselves from the other person. Give and take relationships strongly feature this mutual type of growth.

You do not need to close the door on every one-sided relationship, but you have the right to ask for more from the ones that are currently failing you. Let the other person know that you need their love and support. They may not even realise that they have neglected you, because they are too caught up in their own life. Good relationships are too valuable to just give up on.

Always try to communicate with the other person, as this allows the opportunity for both to discuss what may be simply missed or overlooked in the relationship. A great communication is paramount for two people to be able to solve problems and issues when they arise. In every moment of every relationship, there will always be some sort of constraint or difference that needs to be resolved.

No relationship is perfect, there will always be ups and downs, whether you like it or not. Simply because we are two unique individuals, with separate intelligences and minds. One way or another, you and your partner will encounter many confrontations and arguments during your relationships. With every disagreement, you endure frustration, where there will moments of conflicting behaviours between you and your partner. You will want to unload all your frustrations and anger upon your partner by raising your voice and using foul language when you lose your sense of calmness. In making your point of view this way, you are satisfying your own ego. This behaviour does not help the situation, you are only escalating and adding fuel to the fire of the disagreement.

When this happens, the trick is to become aware of the whole situation and not to encourage or feed your ego with deliberate pride or feeling of righteousness. Respond by listening and not reacting. By holding your 'tongue' and surrendering the creation of any conflict, and by listening to your partner's different views, you will be a much calmer and more poised person. The ability to view others opinion's with an open perspective, will benefit you and your partner and help you walk through the disagreements more harmoniously with mutual discussion.

But you know it is hard to compose yourself when you are triggered by the other person in a heated argument. Right? But the idea is, do not stoop to their level, as that is what they intend you to do. Always keep yourself in check by being consciously aware of yourself, or how you need to state your opposing views to the other person. Do not be absorbed into your partner's reactions or their inappropriate behaviour or views. Just focus on yourself and be aware of 'how' you need to respond. When you do this, your partner will take notice of your calm response and will change their reactions to be in tune with yours.

With a mind that is calm, clear and open to listening, you can always compromise and end the arguments by helping to solve each other's differences, and hence, working towards creating solutions to both problems. Also, by recognising the need to say 'sorry' and forgive one another after settling your differences, you make peace with yourself and your partner where any hurt may have been inflicted during the argument. When this is achieved, both individuals are growing and expanding together in a loving and supporting relationship. By learning from one another and also from within, you are helping to bring the best in each other.

For further effective ways to help you to heal and sustain a lasting, loving and to be more appreciative in a short or long-term relationship or in a marriage, can be explored through an exercise workbook: http://tinyurl.com/mmmgt4y.

If the relationship is destructive or dangerous, then step aside and seek help. No one has the right to take away your freedom of choice and your right to feel safe. Real love between two people should not be infringed by any act of physical violence or any form of abuse that intentionally harms the other.

Unfortunately, I have gone through violent relationships myself in the past. I know what it is like to feel tortured by deliberate shaming and of cruelty. This has left me feeling unworthy and with a sense of helplessness, becoming a very frightened and vulnerable person with no self-confidence, which burdened me for many years. Now, from going through such terrible experiences, I carry battle scars, but I have learned why these things happened and I am now a much stronger person, feeling liberated and with the strength of will to live the life I truly deserve and loving myself with confidence. As of now,

I am willingly to share my love with the right partner, equally to give and take in full love and appreciation.

Simply put, if there is any form of physical or verbal violence in your relationship, then this should not be condoned, for this is not love, but is toxic. It is better to let go of the violence and the unhealthy relationship than to let it consume your life, crippling your health and well-being. I know that it is very hard initially to leave a relationship, especially when you still have feelings and the love for the other person who continues to act wrongly by you. But you have to remember that no destructive love is worth the risk of destroying one's life, which has been created by another.

The early signs are usually evident in the beginning of the relationship, whether toxic or not. The common signs are aggression and defiant control of, and obsession for the other partner. This is what I have experienced and was aware of in the beginning of my past relationship. If the relationship is not a give and take situation that is healthy for both participants involved, then it is not a relationship worth saving.

Clearly, this type of relationship is not worth wasting your time and energy on, let alone spending your life and future with someone who does not care about you. The last thing you want in your life is a relationship that is mentally, physically and spiritually degrading, effectively crippling your sense of self-worth. To succumb to such a feeling of defeat and unhappiness from a loveless life, leads to a state of self-deprivation and depression.

I know this all sounds too depressing already, but hey, when you have been caught up in this unhealthy and toxic relationship like I was, unaware of why I was caught up in it, you need to become aware of the hazardous relationship situation. It was not until finally, I awoke to the realisation that I did not want to feel miserably sad anymore, constantly drowning in my own sorrows in self-punishment and self-pity that I was able to change and had choices. By being aware of the moment and the terrible state I was in, instead of reacting negatively but responding to my situation and deciding that enough was enough, I made the choice to change my life.

With willpower, strength and determination, I courageously walked out of my very long-term tumultuous relationship, leaving it in the past. How amazing it was to feel with such liberation, eliminating the weight from my shoulders and feeling a breath of glorious fresh air. I felt like I was alive again!

In any relationship, I strongly stress do not allow others to corrupt your mind, body and soul. If your partner's demeaning ways or desire for control has changed your overall well-being to suit his or her liking, then you need not participate. Their overbearing need to feel superior and control you clearly reveals that they are insecure themselves, afraid of losing something that they never owned.

Consequently, the reason for their desire for power over their partner's life is to feel adequate in the relationship themselves, and is a case of the need to reinforce their ego and feelings of power, and to overcome issues of insecurity. These are probably related to their past history, perhaps their early life and treatment by other influences or personal factors. Usually, they have been abused or forcibly taken advantage of by someone from their past. Unfortunately, this has detrimental behavioural and psychological effects, corrupting their use of control and possibly causing them to use physical force in the wrong manner, for they did not know or understand any better.

When that person is mistreating you and abusing your trust with their constant lies and deceptive ways, they are also lying to themselves and damaging the relationship. You do not need to waste any of your time and energy with an untrustworthy partner, for they do not deserve you.

A genuine give and take loving relationship should be firmly grounded on complete truth and high values and nothing less. Take note of the other person's values and of their integrity, whether their values are aligned with yours should be distinguishable early in the relationship. Question them on their views of values and integrity, basing your level of trust on their actions. Never settle for less than you are worth and do not compromise your integrity or values.

Importantly, try to recognise these traits in your partner first and foremost before establishing any serious bond in the relationship. If you are embarking on a new relationship, this will help you to save yourself from getting involved in a deliberate unsatisfying, hurtful and unhappy life down the track, with the wrong person. And there is nothing you want from a relationship where trust is either misused or absent. Being in a situation where there is no remorse or respect for one another, clearly shows a very destructive and unhealthy relationship for both parties involved.

It is more worthwhile to be with someone who is going to love you as much as you love them, unconditionally. Your partner should be supportive in every aspect of an affectionate, trusting and loving give and take partnership, with respect and acceptance of all that you are as a whole person. And, likewise, vice versa. After all, you do deserve a reciprocal, trustworthy, loving, and caring relationship, as this truly reflects who you are. Everyone deserves a loving partner and a relationship with kind, honest and caring treatment for a long, loving future together.

The same can be said if someone who simply takes and does not give anything in return. This tells of someone who only thinks of himself or herself, making no or little effort to compromise by contributing their time, let alone giving much love in return. Their selfish acts are intended to prolong their own advancement and no one else. This shows that actions speak louder than words. You can constantly demonstrate your love and affection towards the other person by giving them all your attention, loving embraces and closeness, but receiving little from their end, their non-reciprocal ways will only leave you feeling you have been somewhat cheated or short-changed. There is nothing worse than to be running on a misleading and empty love relationship.

Always value yourself and know what you deserve, and that is definitely not to allow another to use or abuse your kindness and affection for their own advantage. Save your precious love to share with someone who truly appreciates all that you are, and your efforts to give and receive love equally. You should expect the same of your partner to build a sturdy reciprocal and loving relationship.

Make sure your relationships are always a two-way street. Giving frequently and sharing your love equally will create a strong, everlasting bond between yourself and your partner. Importantly, giving and receiving are the essence of a mutual, balanced give and take relationship. This is more so in the whole area of understanding the application and action of *gratitude* for one another. How you use your words in acknowledgement and appreciation of all that your partner has done with their kind gestures. These gestures may not need to be large, little kind gestures have just as much impact, and make all the difference (e.g. thanking your partner when they make you a cup of tea or coffee).

It is unfortunate with many relationships these days, we tend to take each other for granted so easily that we overlook gratitude for their smallest actions. You probably can relate to this. Or you have seen this demonstrated in your friends and family's relationships? I admit that I have learned from past relationships at one stage or another where I had taken everything good in my life for granted, including my partner. It is not until I learned to understand and appreciate myself that I could see things in others and in everything around me to be grateful for.

Honestly, this truly speaks about yourself more than anything else. If you appreciate yourself, then you recognise and appreciate others, as well as their kind gestures, great or small. I strongly believe the action of gratitude is the missing link or ultimate key to sustaining a successful give and take relationship, which epitomises the genuine meaning of love.

Understanding the application of gratitude in your relationship and in your partner every time, every minute, every day, enhances your appreciation of life in general by fulfilling yourself as a more grateful and lovable human being. Remember to always be grateful for who you are and how you love to appreciate others, regardless how annoying their behaviours maybe, and to just be grateful for them as that person. Focusing on appreciating all the goodness of your partner will only draw in more love and care towards them and yourself.

Know that a grateful, healthy, happy and successful relationship, is effortlessly driven by two people. With constant appreciation, compromise, honesty and patience and a will to listen and openly learn and grow from one another, you are on the path to make any relationship succeed!

Creating a true, loving relationship is an acceptance of divine *commitment* to mutual love; to the *courage* to expand, learn and grow endlessly with hearts that are open to one another; to express *compassion* from the heart and soul to unify one's deepest intentions of love and kindness. All of this evolves to a profound *conscious* awareness in all forms of loving communication and action. As a result, you will experience an abundance of happiness when you are involved in a give and take balanced relationship.

One important thing that many people fail to understand or recognise is that there are many different types of relationships in our lives. We all have that friend we love to hang out with, but who is not the most reliable person. Then there are friends that we hate to love, who can be quite annoying, but we are inclined to accept them for who they are and let them just be. Importantly, giving love, respect and appreciation to such friends is more than you can count on having!

It is very sad to see so many great friendships fall apart due to silly misunderstandings. As with any other relationships, taking good care of your friendships helps both you and your friend to grow as respectful, loving individuals. As long as there is a balance between the characters in our life, then each friendship has its own special meaning and each one is fulfilling in its own way.

5. Give to the Less Fortunate!

Another way to give love to the world is by being charitable to those who are less fortunate than you. There are many incredible charities out there that are trying to improve people's lives with the little resources they have available. You can make a difference by donating things in your home that you are not using or by volunteering some of your time to make their mission a little easier. Something that means so little to your life could mean the world to someone else who is suffering.

Giving to charities is a gratifying experience, helping others to improve their lives, especially the poor, and knowing that you are making a difference in this world. Help out wherever you can, with donations or your time for good causes. I love supporting charities that improve the lives many underprivileged children in third world countries and helping to alleviate poverty worldwide.

For me, today's children are tomorrow's future and, given that I have come from a very poor country that was in turbulence after the Vietnam war, I know what it is like to go through such poverty as a child. I believe that children do not deserve a life of no hope and no future just because they are living in poverty.

Support charities that resonate or mean something to you, where you believe supporting that charity will benefit the way you intend and make a significant difference to children's and other's lives…it is very worthwhile!

Give your time to those charities you are passionate about and help make changes for others in need. But if you are too busy and have little time, support wherever you can by donating to those charities, whether your donation is for Children in Poverty, Sick Kids, Breast Cancer, Multiple Sclerosis, Homeless People, or Foodbank for Flood Victims, it will all be worthwhile.

Any form of giving makes a big difference, not only to yourself, because it feels rewarding and fulfilling to be able to contribute to the efforts being made to change situations and lives for the better. Unfortunately, many people are selfishly absorbed in their own self and spending, but are not appreciative enough to see that they have more than others who really need help, and to see what the gift of giving means.

If you are financially struggling at times like this when most are doing it hard to survive, the smallest gestures and contributions go a long way. Even though you may not know it, people will help you out in your worst times and when you are in financial need. Regardless of how much wealth you have, situations may suddenly arise and change your family and circumstances. For instance, a very wealthy family can be encumbered with financial bankruptcy, and need to seek support from relatives and friends, or outside, or even community support to help them financially get back on their feet, and there will always be benevolent people out there to help other people in need of financial support. Conversely, a very poor family can be open to new found of help and financial rewards and opportunities for better options of lifestyle.

> Giving gives a new form of life and real meaning to the gift of generosity and in receiving – the ebb and flow of continuous abundance. — Natasha Dao

You do not have to be rich to be generous. If he has the spirit of true generosity, a pauper can give like a prince. — Corrine V. Wells

Most people do not really understand what it is like to be poor to the extent that they are truly suffering. It is hard for people who have not experienced it to understand what it would be like if you could not afford enough food or even shelter. Could you imagine not being able to afford a loaf of bread or a bottle of milk? There is probably enough loose change in your couch cushions to scrape together a couple bucks for a hot meal, yet so many people go without.

Unfortunately, there are many people all over the world who are suffering from poverty every single day and they yearn for such luxuries as a hot meal, clean water or a warm bed to sleep in. They do not have proper health care, a solid education or aspirations that they have a bright future ahead of them. These are simple things that we may take for granted in our own lives, but they seem unobtainable to people all over the world.

It is important that you always remember how lucky you are to have the life that you do. Be grateful for everything you currently have: access to clean, hot and drinking water every day, the ability to consume all sorts of foods that we can buy from the supermarket, clean and fresh clothes keeping us warm and dressed, and having a roof over our heads, providing us with comfort and security. With gratitude and appreciation for every day, you are a living breathe of life, in good health in mind, body and spirit, and you can truly count your blessings for living an abundant life on this earth! So make your life a worthwhile — a fulfilled life! As some would say: 'Carpe Diem!'. (Seize the day!) Or, 'Savour every precious moment of your life, all your senses, and be fully aware of your surroundings — live in the moment'.

Look at the extreme poverty that so many innocent children are experiencing in third world countries. Their pain and desperation is unimaginable to anyone who is fortunate enough to have never endured a day living in such uncertainty. They do not care about the hottest video game, the latest iPhone or the brand name label that is sewn into the back of their shirt. They are living day by day, just to survive.

Yet, there are so many people and children in thriving countries who have little appreciation of what they have, and an abundance of everything is offered to them. In such countries, surplus food is wasted and over consumerism is prevalent, and people can selfishly indulge in whatever they want. They take granted for their own existence and the presence of others for love and support, especially their birth parents, guardians or friends. Sadly, appreciation for each other is taken for granted on a daily basis.

By widening your vision, and feeling gratitude for your everyday life, you can see that you have more than what you really need. In thinking of others and of those less fortunate, who are struggling through everyday poverty and destruction, you can appreciate the meaning of life and its true value. Open your heart to others with, caring and compassion by giving a hand to others in need, whether it be giving your time or a donation, will help you to fulfil your own sense of self love and compassion, and align and resonate with others, or simply give you time to bathe in each other's presence and share a moment.

Helping the less fortunate does not only refer to assisting those who are suffering due to a lack of financial wealth. It also includes individuals suffering from medical issues, anyone who is drowning in despair, people who are afflicted with loneliness or have gone through a bereavement or loss. They may not be looking for spare change or a donation, but they need support, comfort and encouragement just as desperately. They are in need of a friend or a companion, or maybe they just need someone to talk to or who is willing to listen and help them through a rough patch.

Giving your love, attention and support to others is the best medicine you can give towards curing another's disease. By bringing them happiness through a simple smile, the loving gesture of a friendly and warm embrace, or showing them how much you care for them by means of loving actions and kindness, can truly help people's lives to flourish again.

> *Without Love, life fades and dies. Where as with Love, life flourishes and is lived. — Natasha Dao*

Bring a little sunshine into the world!

Try to always walk around with a big smile on your face and a kind word for everyone you know. Happiness starts when you are ready to give your love freely and it should show in even the simplest things that you do. Be ready to inspire and to encourage anyone who crosses your path. Your positive attitude will be contagious and it will spread a little sunshine into even the cloudiest of lives. You will also feel your own personal reward when you realise that you have brightened the life of someone else.

Your exuberance and upbeat energy, resonating with internal and external happiness, will attract others and they will naturally be drawn to your positive vibes. Not only people will see or sense your energy in having that so-called a 'zest for life' and 'feel good' connection in everything you do of actions, but more importantly, you will be spreading the vibration of love which is the meaning of internal bliss and happiness for others to receive. Whether you express it through the physical and affectionate embrace of hugs; verbal kindness and caring communication, or simply in the acknowledgement of other's presence.

Whether you help others by volunteering, donating or simply by smiling when you see them, your presence will have a positive impact on someone else's life. The world is full of people who experience tough challenges and serious struggles, so that anything you can do to counter act the destruction is a great way to give back to society. So reach out and help someone who may be going through a rough time.

Giving of your time and generosity is a blessing and a gift you can give to another. There are so many people out there who need your help, and every little thing you can do truly makes a difference in their lives. A little bit of change from your pocket won't make a difference in your life, but when it is combined with so many other people's change, it can create a world of difference!

Raising substantial amount of money, whether big or small, for a good cause or charity, through personal events or community or corporate functions is more than enough, and knowing you will have an impact on others' lives who have less than yourself. Your actions will set firm grounds for others to also help and support your good intentions in this world.

> *To get you must Give. I've scarce enough bread, and of course one must live; but I would partake of life's bountiful store....Then you must Give more. As he gave of himself in useful living, then joy crowned his days, for he grew rich in Giving. — Arthur William Beer*

No matter how small or insignificant you feel that your effort may be, it is still a step in the right direction. No one person can change the world, but if everybody tries to be a little less selfish and give of themselves freely, together we can really make the world a better place to live. In acting out of selflessness and not selfishness, you will serve your own gratification and self-fulfilment, by helping and doing incredible deeds for others who need help the most. This reflects one's measure of nobility and humility. Realise how fortunate you actually are in your own life and share it with those who need it more than you.

Be generous, be giving, behold the gift to know the meaning of receiving. The total act of inner appreciation. — Natasha Dao

6. Sharing Your Positive Attitude

One great way to give love to the world is by sharing your positive attitude with the people in your life. It sounds simple, but the way you act and react to everyday situations can have a huge impact on your life. If you try to find the bright side in everything that happens, you will quickly learn that every cloud really does have a silver lining. The key to finding it starts with having the right perspective.

'Be the best and wholesome person you can and as onto others.'

'Live life to the fullest and don't take anything for granted, by LOVING life with ultimate COMPASSION.'

'Embrace; love; life and celebrate!'

— Natasha Dao

Maintaining a positive attitude is an important part of finding an abundance of happiness within your life, but it is more important that you express it outwardly, so that you are setting a positive example for others to follow. Having a positive mindset also allows you to draw better outcomes and opportunities towards you, and attract like-minded people into your life.

Every negative can be transformed into a positive. It is just a matter of acknowledging the positive outlook or solution to every problem or negativity. Like I always say when encountering any obstacles or problems: 'If there is a will, then there is a way!' Essentially, do not focus on the problem, but on solving it instead. Well, at least, in most cases this is how I like to look at it. A positive attitude can be just as contagious as a negative attitude, so it is important that you choose your mood wisely.

Have you ever noticed how someone with a bad attitude can spoil the mood for everyone around them?

Negativity can spread like wildfire. Fortunately, a positive attitude has the same power. If you are upbeat, energised and ready for a good time, then this will inspire the same response in other people. You have a choice of what kind of role you want to play in society. If you decide to demonstrate love, self-confidence, joy and happiness, then you can have a positive effect on the people who choose to follow your example.

Your positive energy will resonate with others when they are in your presence. Like a strong magnetic force, people will be drawn towards your feel-good energy, which will provide them with happy, loving vibes, and who doesn't want to feel like this? Right? I certainly do! But don't get me wrong, sometimes it is not natural to be constantly positive 24/7. The human psyche is wired to have a balance of opposites. As long as you are aware of what causes the thoughts and actions that create negative outcome. By rectifying the problem, which already has a negative outcome, with a different outlook and a positive conscious action, you can change the outcome to a better one.

There is nothing worse than being negative about everything in life, for life is just too short! Or even in associating with people who are down in the dumps with themselves and are constantly complaining about all parts of life! I bet you know several of these people, just as I have encountered them as past friends. Sometimes without realising it, we succumb to their negative outputs with negative behaviours and thinking ourselves ….this I call 'Stink'n think'n'.

As long as we are aware of how others are negatively impacting us, we can adjust and change from a negative into a positive perspective. Instead of allowing others to have a bad influence on us, we should initiate a positive influence on them to help change their negative ways and be a role model. Being positive always has a benevolent influence on others; in no time, others will cotton on to this style of action, the state of being constantly happy, open-minded, finding win–win solutions to every problem, minor or major, and always having a bright outlook on life, regardless of what happens!

Optimism is the epitome mindset to grow and expand personally as to live for a brighter, fulfilled future. — *Natasha Dao*

One way of helping ourselves to become more aware and in set in motion a program of positive thinking is by applying a daily positive 'feeling' chart list, which will help us focus on how we are feeling and in describing one positive word for the day. Every day has a new positive word for at least 21 days. This will help to effectively program our mind to be positive in its thinking and in action through the expression of writing positive words. Implement your daily positive 'feeling' chart on the next page.

21-DAY DAILY POSITIVE FEELING CHART

DESCRIPTION FEELING WORDS	MONDAY	TUESDAY	WEDNESDAY	THURSDAY	FRIDAY	SATURDAY	SUNDAY
1	grateful	happy	liberated	.....	.....	.....	.....
3							
5							
7							
9							
11							
13							
15							
...							
21							

In fact, you can really change your situations and outcomes to be whatever you would like them to be. Keeping in mind how you are reading the problem, your perceptions can provide solutions by keeping in mind the power of positive thinking. This trains us to have a healthy and balanced mind, consistently seeing positive solutions to any situations that may arise in life. It creates challenges to invigorate and give interest to our lives, and self-growth in this area teaches us to walk confidently through both big and small triumphs, trials and tribulations.

Another way of spreading your positivity is by having a brighter outlook that can change the world, one person at a time, simply by sharing a smile. Greet every person you pass with a warm smile and it will ignite a blaze of smiles. The people who see you will return the smile to the next person they see, and it will be passed from person to person. This then will have a ripple effect of brightening people's day with a simple gesture.

Have you not come across people that do not want to look upwards, but keep their eyes down to avoid looking when they pass someone? It is sad to see so many people rarely smile but frown with tension and possibly stress written all over their faces when in public. Instead, by displaying a happy face in the presence of others, you are radiating inner happiness that others can feel. Either way, people will sense the warmth and vibrancy shining from your face, the glow of internal happiness that radiates brightly.

A smile is a curve that sets everything straight.

Self-confidence is also contagious. If you believe in yourself, spread that feeling to others who may not be feeling as confident about their own life. Show them that if you have a 'can do' attitude, then you really can do anything you set your mind to. It may take some hard work, but odds are it will be worth it. Do not pay any attention to people who doubt your capabilities. Your positivity needs to be strong enough to overpower any negativity that tries to shake your foundation.

Walk tall, demonstrating pride and self-liberation. Your positive actions and appearance to others and to yourself creates self-confidence for others to be inspired by, or to willingly follow. Always set a good example in a positive way as a great leader or influencer. Always treat others with -respect and dignity, just as you would like to be treated. Give people the benefit of the doubt, without any form of judgement. Accept them for who they are, without hesitating because of differences of culture or background, religion and belief, colour of skin, hair, age or superficial outlook.

Importantly, change your thoughts, and your mind will shift to a constructive and positive perception of life overall. Like everything you do in your life, whether with good intentions or not, the universe will in return provide you what you are projecting outwards. If you feel anger and hatred towards the world, most likely you will encounter individuals or experiences that are also bitter and angry about their life. Because you have deeply succumbed to your own negative outlook on life, you will be unable to see anything else, thus attracting only the same kind of energy.

On the other hand, if you are comparatively carrying out your life in the tune of content happiness and doing good for others in love and gratitude. You are most likely to attract more of such people and circumstances that melodically flows within to your tune. Another perspective you can learn about yourself is by simply looking at what you are attracting and drawing into your life.

Don't you just get annoyed when you come across someone who is grumpy and angry about their life and are brimming with negative energy? Well, this encounter is not a mere coincidence, but a personal projection of a lesson to be learned about yourself. So take account of who and in what circumstances this takes place, so you can understand the reasons it happened. Such lessons are for your advancement, to help your growth. The multitude of such personal experiences that I have encountered throughout my life, have taught me many life lessons, and to become the wiser person that I believe I am today. So do not ever dismiss any little experiences that you are not happy with or how you are feeling, for what you are resonating will be the creation of those experiences.

Given that said, it is always best to create a happy, positive and loving environment for yourself and others to bring upon yourself the exact fulfilment of your intentions.

Change your thoughts. Change your life. — Dr Wayne Dyer

If you feel good about life, pass it on, so others can feel just as good! Share your smile, share words of encouragement and pass on your positive attitude to as many people as possible. If everyone starts off in a good mood, there will be no avenue for a negative vibe to creep in. Remember, a positive attitude will bring positive results!

Look at how you can create more positive impact into your life, work and social well-being: http://tinyurl.com/lvgjxzb.

49

7.   Give of Yourself!

You do not need to show physical or emotional love to everyone you meet, but it is important that you freely give of your time and of yourself. You may not have the financial means to be generous, but that does not mean you do not have value that you can offer to the world. Love does not have to be given in the form of a material object; in fact, the best gifts of love are free and unconditional.

> *Love within from the heart, embellishes such great joy and happiness where only one can feel deeply remotely natural to give with all to another.*
> *— Natasha Dao*

Sharing your love, care and contentment with others shows that you are amplifying your love by allowing it to shine whole-heartedly outwards and into people's life. It is the best feeling you can experience. Uplifting them, bringing their vulnerabilities to the surface and replacing them with positive feeling and embracing the magic of the love you share with them. When this happens, you can only feel from the heart and demonstrate the actions of love freely, with tenderness and kindness for each other.

The amazing freedom to express yourself by giving love to others, brings about the gentle 'goodness' of caring for yourself that is projected beautifully onto the receiver. Love is the greatest gift you can give of yourself to others. Be open to giving and receiving love with whomever you come across every day, regardless of who they are. Whether it is a conversation with your next-door neighbour, time spent with friends in the park, a friendly smile or a 'Hi' to a passer-by from your front yard, laughter and joyful moments with your family, or intimacy and nurturing affection with that special partner.

Always look at ways to give yourself in the authenticity of the whole meaning of love. There is never enough in sharing of the humanity of love around this world, so start with your own.

> *Love with without prejudice, give the virtue of continuous acceptance to everyone and to yourself, no less than to others to love freely. For love is endless, provokingly generous to give by many and absolutely everyone infectiously worldwide. — Natasha Dao*

You can give someone a kind word, an encouraging pep talk, a meaningful embrace or a passionate kiss to show your love. You can also give compliments or a shoulder to lean on. Any gesture when you share yourself freely in an attempt to better someone else's world counts! By doing something kind for someone else, you are essential giving them a piece of yourself.

You are the greatest gift you can give to the world!

Giving of yourself is easy for you to do and it will not cost you a single penny. All it takes is a willingness to share who you are with the people who are in your life. You cannot get any easier than that! Plus, when you willingly give of yourself, you will reap your own emotional reward, because you will instantly feel good about having a positive effect on someone else's life. It will boost your own self-worth and it will inspire you to continue giving.

You should also give your talents freely in an effort to improve the world. If you can sing, then join a choir. If you are good with children, you should volunteer to be a mentor. If you can cook, then volunteer at your local mission to help feed the homeless people in your community. Use your talents to make the world a better place and you will feel the pride and self-satisfaction that natural follows any selfless act.

I was blessed by meeting several motivational influences who inspired me to follow my dreams and set high goals for myself. In return, I reach out to others who are struggling and I try to give them the encouragement and support to find happiness in their own lives. It takes very little effort and the ripple effect that it creates will touch more lives than I ever could possible do on my own.

> *The wheel of life keeps turning so what you give or take will eventually come back to you. Make sure you look forward to it's arrival. — Sally Eichhorst*

Everyone has something special that they can share with the world and it would be a waste to keep it hidden behind a cloud of modesty or self-doubt. Be proud of yourself and take pride in everything you do, for you are blessed with talents to serve others and for the rest of the world to receive. Be no less than you are intended to be, the greatest and best possible self. Never settle for a life of mediocrity.

Most people are comfortably settled in their average daily jobs without understanding who they truly are, or how best to use their highest given talents and skills. They accept their life as a simple means to get by and nothing more. They are happy to be enslaved by their jobs with an unfulfilling lifestyle or without wanting to achieve any more or a much more gratifying and fulfilling purpose.

This is similar to how I felt in my last corporate job, many years back, and many of my colleagues were in this same situation. Unhappy in their jobs, but they still adhered to the notion of the obligatory bills, mortgages and life responsibilities. Hence, many chose to be where they were and created their own circumstances, whether they were good or bad life choices.

Fortunately, unlike others, I woke up to myself and realised there is much more meaning to my life. The sense of a fulfilling and enriching purpose for the self. I intuitively knew I was made on earth to do much greater good for humanity and for the world. My career was a vehicle in my journey to help me discover my true purpose in life, like this mission of spreading the message of love and gratitude and self-empowerment through means of this book.

After all, like everything else in life, there are always choices. Just beware of the choices you make, keeping in mind the choices that are best suited to your higher purpose. You know you are capable of anything in life when you set your mind intentionally and with an open heart to a genuine goal.

I believe everyone is here on earth to serve a profound higher purpose of who they are and to give to others. For instance, I believe I was meant to write this book, to bring forth a message of love and gratitude and of self-empowerment to share with everyone. Helping people to learn, grow and develop into more loving souls and in appreciation and gratitude to enrich their lives, by empowering and inspiring others on their transformational journey to find their true higher purpose or life-awakening calling. All of this is within reach through the healing provided when we open ourselves to our inner love and gratitude and allow it to flow into all aspects of life, to find inner peace, self-love, freedom and all to the abundance of life and happiness.

Overall, aim to create a world conscious of love, peace, unity and harmony for all humankind.

8.   Give Laughter!

There is a reason why people say that laughter is the best medicine. Surprisingly, there are as many health benefits to laughing as there are emotional rewards. Laughter has been proven to improve your circulation, lower your blood pressure, boost your immune system and increase your overall life expectancy. By laughing, you are medically releasing the hormones in your brain colloquially called 'the happy drugs' or, more formally, 'endorphins'. Laughter will help you reduce your stress levels and will improve your outlook on life. It also works your abdomen and core stomach muscles, so it is a phenomenally fun workout.

Now, who does not enjoy laughing to the point of hysteria, with pains in the stomach and swelling watery eyes? I certainly have and really love to laugh whenever I can! It is like watching someone making a complete fool of themselves unintentionally or watching an extremely funny comedy on tv.

A good example is when I reflect back on seeing my aunt walking into a glass door without shattering any glass (thank goodness!) or doing serious damage to herself, other than our family in hysteria laughing at her. All of which indicates an uncontrolled feeling of joy and happiness. And there is nothing wrong with laughing yourself senseless and silly. You cannot help but to just laugh at every circumstance that arises. On the plus side, laughter is infectious and anyone can easily be provoked of such wonderful feelings of actions.

It is unfortunate these days that many people are not able to be silly or cheerful enough to accept the invitation to laughter. The seriousness of people's careers, finances and family stresses, reduces their time to find happiness in laughing. Laughter is only natural and normal to do on a daily basis. After all, what does this tell you of the society and the scope of the idiocy of the world in needing to pay money to attend laughing classes?! Now I think that is crazy enough to laugh about!

The best trigger for the laughter or happiness inside you is to stand in front of the mirror and practise of smiling at yourself. I know this sounds quite strange and silly, but hey, as a positive start to your day in making yourself feel good, there is nothing queer about it, I assure you. Smiling to yourself every day in the mirror brings out the happy and vibrant self, ready to laugh at any possibilities that unfold during the day.

Have you ever been in a situation where the worst has taken place, like a birthday event where you have devoted all of your time and energy in organising the perfect momentous day for everyone to experience. However, nothing goes according to plan, and you experience disaster after disaster, especially when the cake was dropped on the floor! In the end, all I did was laugh at the whole ordeal. I thought the destroyed birthday cake was somehow hilarious, after overcoming my worries; I just burst out laughing senselessly.

To laugh at any and every circumstance that life presents you with is the best and most healthy way to approach a more cheerful self, and have a pleasant and happy outlook on your life. By laughing, you are helping to provoke a much clearer and happy mindset to make any decisions to be suitably right in every situation to work. Laugh as much as you can! Life is too short otherwise!

Not everything in life is going to go your way and there will be embarrassing incidents that you will want to quickly forget. Instead of allowing these slips up to push us into hiding, try to view them as a chance for you to learn how to laugh at yourself. Being able to take something that made you look silly and then turning it into a great story that you can share with your friends and family is priceless. You will be surprised at how many embarrassing moments that seemed devastating at the time end up will end up being some of your favourite stories to share. Being able to share a funny story is a great way to spread laughter and, ultimately, give your love to the rest of the world.

Love everything and everyone; Release all judgement and resistance; Allow yourself to just be joyful...regardless of what happens. — Harrison Klein

Either way I have learned to laugh at all my mishaps. I have ripped my skirt in public, I've dumped coffee in my lap at work and I've tripped over my own two feet in a less than graceful way when people were watching, but I don't let any of it stop me. I would quickly make a joke out of my clumsiness and I would laugh just as hard as anyone else who saw my fumble. Embarrassing stuff happens to everyone and there is no reason to let it bother you. As long as no one gets hurt, silly slip-ups are always worth a good laugh!

Laughter gives us distance. It allows us to step back from an event, deal with it and then move on.
— Bob Newhart

Bringing laughter into your everyday life is a fantastic way to positively enhance your personal well-being under any circumstances, effectively enlivening others as well as yourself. Give your family, friends or even strangers something silly to laugh about. We can all do with spreading love and laughter to enrich our souls with joy and happiness, we deserve to enjoy our less stressed and dull lives. Be free to laugh out loud, wherever you are. This is also known as releasing the internal 'chi' for a healthy mind and body energy outflow. Do not be afraid or embarrassed about projecting your voice with laughter. If your laugh sounds like a hickory donkey or a crazy hyena, who really cares, right? As long as you are enjoying yourself laughing silly and having fun that is what matters most.

Laughter should come naturally, and it is usually inspired by meaningful moments of gratitude. It is always best shared freely, without hesitation or reservation. You can give love to anyone by sharing your sense of humour and your laughter any time the opportunity arises.

You will experience magical health benefits, you will improve your own mood and, hopefully, you will also lift other people's spirits in the process. So just let yourself to be free, frivolous and laugh out loud silly!

9.   Give Compliments

Everyone likes to be complimented, even if they shrug it off or act as though they do not deserve it. I promise you that they are still happy that you said it, no matter what the reaction is at first. It is always a nice feeling to have our appearance, our talents or our hard work recognised or praised. It is especially nice when we are not expecting it or when it comes from an unlikely source.

Giving compliments is an act of being intentionally and personally positive. Whether it is in the form of kind words or actions to be given to another, compliments truly exemplify genuine love and care for the receiver. This expression of love should not be limited by the right time to do so or to specific individuals who we think deserve it. Giving compliments is a genuine act of love and should be randomly shared and freely willed to many.

Do not be afraid to give compliments openly and freely to strangers (e.g. initiating an admiring compliment to a pair of passing joggers whose bright-coloured sneakers have caught your eyes). By giving them smiles and words, they can mirror back with their appreciation by saying 'Thank you'. In return, both from giving the compliment and from the receiver's end, both parties will create a happy and loving vibrational feel for one another. Not only I am creating myself to feel happy by giving the compliment, which was spontaneous, but making others feel the same as well.

Now, do not tell me that nobody likes to be complimented with a nice smile and kind words once in awhile? I know you do and I certainly do! We all love to have positive feedback now and then. This helps us to open ourselves freely to experience in giving and receiving love, with resulting feelings of happiness. The positive effect of such emotions is to boost our desire to give love to others by giving compliments to them, rewarding them with loving recognition.

Be always open to either give or receive compliments freely. We all know how this feels from both ends, for we have all experienced compliments one way or another. Giving others compliments, is a great feeling, and I am very comfortable with this and love to do so. Every compliment is directed with genuine loving intentions. It makes me feel good and happy to see others' faces beaming with delightful surprise in appreciation of my recognition and kind words. Showing that I do very much care for them will certainly leave them feeling wonderfully happy with themselves.

Sharing your love through giving compliments on a daily basis is profoundly fulfilling and triggers happiness, especially in a romantic partner or a husband and wife relationship. By continually commenting appreciatively on each other and showing how much you love the other person with your actions, you set a positive direction for the expansion of a very loving, nurturing and happy relationship. Sometimes actions without words are not constructive enough to reinforce the love and care you feel for the other person so that it carries an authentic meaning of love. Conversely, words without actions are meaningless, for actions speak louder than words.

Your partner can affectionately demonstrate their constant love for you with kind and caring words such as 'I love how you care enough to care about me in everything you do for me'. These simple, yet poignant words can also uplift the other person so they feel strongly the love and support they have for their partner. Words and how you deliver them can have a powerful impact when you give compliments to your partner. Not only does this strengthen your devotion, and the love and attention sought by both partners in giving and receiving compliments, but it is the same for all compliments, keeping in mind that constant loving appreciation will equate to loving actions.

When someone has put extra effort into their appearance, try to make a point of telling them how nice they look. It takes absolutely no effort on your part and it will make them feel like their effort was worth it. If you have noticed someone has lost some weight, then you should acknowledge their hard work and comment on their new physique. If someone is struggling to make life changes or personal improvements, then your kind words could end up being the very motivation that they need to continue on their new path.

The same positive encouragement should be applied in any employee/employer relationship. When someone has a boss who points out when they have done something well, it will inspire the employee to work harder to receive additional praise. It has been studied and proven that employees who feel appreciated and complimented by their employer are willing to go above and beyond to constantly perform at their best.

Getting a compliment is uplifting! So is giving a compliment!

It never hurts to give someone positive reinforcement. Unfortunately, many people suffer from unfounded self-doubt. They are insecure and they need reassurance from the people in their life, especially from the people that they truly care about. Encouraging someone by recognising their accomplishments or telling them how proud you are of them will reinforce their own belief in themselves.

Giving positive empowering compliments to others helps them to see these aspects in themselves, so they become and change into a better and improved self. Helping to give them more self-confidence and to see in their own capabilities a more worthy person, is the encouragement their pride or ego. Although, there is nothing wrong with bringing out that egocentric side where you can be and feel absolutely proud of your accomplishments and achievements. Such confidence will be reflected in your overall physical appearance, how you speak to others and how you carry yourself.

I was a nervous wreck when I decided to leave my stable career to pursue my dream as a philanthropist author. I posted the decision as my status on Facebook and the outstanding replies of encouragement and support were the final boost I needed to take the next step. There was a part of me that always knew I could do it, but my insecurities kept allowing doubt to creep in. Once I knew that others believed in my future success, my confidence overcame my doubts and I was willing to take the risk. It is always easier to believe in yourself when you feel like others believe in you too.

You can make another person feel good about their life simply by complimenting their appearance, their successes, or their positive attitude. It takes almost no effort and the impact could be huge on someone else's self-confidence! Think about how good you feel when someone compliments you! Why would you not want to give someone else that same uplifting support and encouragement?

Now, that does not mean you should lie and tell someone that they are an incredible singer if their voice sounds like nails on a chalkboard. You do not want to encourage them to try out for American Idol and then have them end up making it on the blooper reel. It is important that you are sincere and that you try to find something that honestly deserves to be complimented. Fake compliments are never necessary and they can sometimes backfire and cause a bigger problem.

If you cannot find something good to say about someone, then don't say anything at all.

Learning to give compliments will also help you to find the good that lies in others. Not only you are pleasing others with genuine and good intentions, you are giving your love and letting them understand how you feel about them, by reinforcing their positive attributes. Everyone has something special that is worth your praise and recognition. You have to see past your difference and try to focus on their more admirable qualities. Sometimes you may need to dig pretty deep to find something special about another person, but you can trust me that everyone has something about them that deserves a compliment.

Here are a few simple sentences that can have a huge impact on someone else's life.

'I love being with you! You are such a positive person!'

'You look great! Did you do something with your hair or had a hair-cut?'

'Wow, that dress looks amazing on you!'

'You did a great job on the presentation today!'

'Your body looks so toned. Have you been working out?'

'Seeing your beautiful smile every morning really starts my day off right!'

'You are so funny. Thank you for always making me laugh!'

Spread happiness, share love and give others sincere compliments freely, as often as possible. You will make other people feel good, which is a fast way to making yourself feel better. There is nothing more uplifting than having the power to lift the spirits of someone else.

When you really think about it, it is pretty easy to come up with something nice to say about another person. So, why not say it out loud? There is no down side, since you are almost guaranteed to be met with a smile in return. It is a powerful way to live and the rewards you will reap are limitless. Giving compliments is a great way to strengthen relations and build happiness in your life and the lives of those around you.

Only the development of COMPASSION and understanding for others can bring us the tranquillity and HAPPINESS we all seek. — Dalai Lama

10.   Share Your Wisdom!

Sometimes in life, your plans do not always go according to schedule, leaving you to go through all sorts of obstacles and hardships in life. For some people it is unfortunate that they might have to learn their life lessons the hard way, rather than from early minor mistakes. One of my terrible experiences and mistakes would have to reflect back to my first relationship, where I learned to understand not to take any good relationships for granted or others for that matter. Not only have I lost the loving, genuine and, at most, trustworthy years of the relationship (however people do change), but the appreciation for what he did for me during all the good times we had together as a loving couple.

More importantly, I have learned to forgive others, as this has helped me to forgive myself in respect of self-healing and letting go of all the resentment and anger I felt with my first partner. Understanding that I need to let go and let it be 'water under bridge', helps me to release all emotional ties with that person so I can move forward with my life.

At first, this was hard for me to grasp and come to terms with, especially when, every day, I was filled with constant hate and rage against him. Forgiving him was the last thing I wanted to do. It was not until I realised that I did not want to feel such anger and hurt, as it was emotionally tiring and literally 'eating' every part of my well-being that I could move on, knowing that person was no longer healthy for my life, and not needing to waste any more of my energy. I harmoniously surrendered to walk out of the relationship, leaving behind me all the emotional tears and pain ... or at least that was what I thought.

Several years down the track, completely unaware of the emotional pain that I was still carrying around brought me back for full closure to my past relationship. From here, we were understanding and diplomatic enough to forgive each other once and for all, even parting as friends. This experience has taught me to learn to love him despite what we had gone through in order to forgive him. Hence, learning to love from my deep compassionate self gave me the ability to forgive myself and, in doing so, to forgive and let go of the past.

Only by going through pain, I mean strenuous gut-wrenching emotional pain; I have come to understand more about myself and who I am as a person. All things happen for a reason and support the notion that life is a series of cause and an effect.

Only through these life lessons and experiences you will learn from your mistakes and grow along the journey to become a wiser and better person. If you find that you are repeating the same mistakes, then there is a reason why this is occurring — possibly the fact that you did not learn the lesson the first, second or third time? Ideally, you do not need to go through this saga of mistakes to figure out what you need to do or make that change for the better too late.

I have shared some of the lessons I learnt from my own relationships and life (which I am sure you probably can also relate to). I can now find inner peace, and self-love and compassionate love to give to others. So it is only wise to make peace with others and within yourself, or with any remaining hurt from past or present relationships to heal and grow personally. Making amends allows you to push forward to a more positive life.

Generally, life is a continuous learning experience and, unfortunately, most of the lessons we learn come from the mistakes that we make. There is no shame in making a mistake. Everyone makes mistakes, but the important thing is to learn from them and pass along the advice to the next generation. Why not try to save the next generation from the same struggles that we endured, by trying to tactfully warn them of potential problems that may arise from their decisions.

You cannot force someone else to change their mind in order to stop them from making a mistake. Sometimes it is a lesson to be learned to help them grow and become a better person and in their decision-making. However, you should still try to give them guidance. You should also try to help them through the experience, if they choose not to follow your advice and end up making the same mistake as you. As someone who has personally survived my share of struggle, I feel I have valuable wisdom to pass onto to others. Hopefully, they listen, but if not I will be there to help pick them back up when they fall.

You should also pass on wisdom when you feel that someone is in trouble. If you encounter any form of abuse, please make sure that you warn as many trustworthy people as possible. It is difficult to speak up when someone is hurting you, but it is crucial in order to prevent future victims. If no one is aware of the problem, then it could go on for years and years without anyone stopping it.

Wisdom is not a product of schooling but of the lifelong attempt to acquire it. — Albert Einstein

Wisdom can come from a variety of sources, but its effects are amplified when it is passed on to someone else. If you have knowledge that can benefit someone else's life, then there is no value holding it inside. Use the information you have gained through your own life experiences to better the lives of anyone and everyone that is within your reach. You have the power to create positive change in someone else's life!

Take for example if you have successfully lost weight and improved your overall health. That is something that you can use to help guide others towards the same success. You know the mental and physical changes you needed to make to succeed and you can pass on your tips to someone else who is struggling with the same problem.

You can also share your wisdom by writing an inspirational or instructional book that is beneficial for the reader. I choose to write this book of empowering positive steps in order to motivate and inspire others to believe in themselves and the goodness in people, and to search for their own happiness through the healing in activating their inner love and gratitude; hence, helping them to find their higher purpose in life.

Another technique is to be inspired with daily powerful wisdom words and phrases to help to invigorate more shares of your own wisdoms along the line of other inspirational wisdom teachings. More ways where you can improve in changing your thoughts and in your life with greater wisdoms. http://tinyurl.com/kj85s6u.

The wisdom I have gained through my hardships and triumphs is the power achieved through healing and by activating my inner love and gratitude into all aspects of life to find inner peace, self-love and freedom. That is why I am giving back by sharing my stories and wisdom to help you take positive steps towards empowering yourself to live the life that you deserve, to find the right path to your goals and dreams of a higher purpose and fulfilment life.

Hindsight is helpful and foresight is a blessing but insight makes wise men wise. — Garry Mac

You can share your wisdom by becoming a teacher, speaker, healer, counsellor, coach, parent or even just a good friend to someone who is feeling a little lost in life. It does not matter how you choose to educate others. The important thing is that you choose to share the wisdom you have gained over the course of your life, so that others can learn from your mistakes and successes. Spreading your knowledge to those who seek it is a powerful way that you can share your love with the world.

Look for Learning Opportunities
In order to find happiness, make an effort to continue to grow and develop your mind. Truly happy people seek out learning opportunities anywhere that they can. There are so many fun and exciting ways for you to expand your current knowledge base, besides reading textbooks or researching information online. You can learn new things by taking a cooking class, visiting an art gallery or even just by listening more closely to people around you.

You should also make the time to attend relevant seminars or take college courses or seek out for self-growth development online products, especially if they have the potential to help you advance in improving yourself or career and in life. My recommendation to help you further understand how powerful the mind of thoughts (human psychology), can actually create the life that you want to fulfil and only dream of living.

https://inspwr.infusionsoft.com/go/breakthrough/a8499

The world is constantly changing and, due to advancements in technology, there will always be new and more efficient developments in how people do business. It is important that you are always willing to continue your academic growth and development, so you stay current with what is going on in the world.

> *Anyone who stops learning is old, whether at twenty or eighty. Anyone who keeps learning stays young. The greatest thing in life is to keep your mind young. — Henry Ford*

I also recommend reading the newspaper or watching the news on television occasionally or when you can. In order to understand the state of our world, it is a good idea to follow current events. Just keep in mind not to be reactive towards all the negative reports, even though in 95% of the news we are constantly bombarded with devastating content! Although, I know this is hard to watch, that is why when I do get the chance to view the news I only reflect on the good news, if there is any. Sometimes it is painful to watch the amount of violence and destruction that is going on, but it will make you more grateful for your own life. It will also show you new opportunities where you can make a positive difference for yourself and for others.

I was watching the news a while back ago and heard about families and children abroad were caught up in natural disasters and were in desperate need of immediate clothing and blankets, or the other alternative was to make a donation. At that time, I did not have much money, but still managed to donate a substantial small amount of $50. I also went through my belongings and clothing or anything that I did not need that I could donate. I organised to sell these things at the Sunday flea markets, forwarding the proceeds to help and support these families and children in need. I ended up raising around $160 for the proceeds! Even though this may seem a small amount, I was very pleased with the result and felt happy to know that I was making a significant difference for these people who really do need the money.

In the overly consumerist society that we live in, I am sure that within every one of our homes we can find unwanted and rarely used items and clothing that we can either directly donate to charitable centres such as Life line or Saint Vincent De Paul. Making a good reason to sell them online or at flea markets and donate the proceeds for any great cause. It only takes a moment for each and one of us to now and then to just stop thinking about ourselves for once and to consider others who are in far worse living conditions and are striving to survive. We can all help and reach out to support these worthy causes or those who are doing it tough in our immediate community and make all the difference that we can.

I would not have known about the natural disaster and the people who were involved if I had not seen the news on TV. I also learned about several other changes and developments in my community, which affected me in other ways. Now that most newspapers and news are available online, there is no excuse not to get the daily reports and stay on top of current affairs. The more you know, the more you grow!

11.   Give a Helping Hand

No one can survive this world completely on their own. Our parents help us with almost everything when we are babies, our teachers guide us through our education and our friends help us shape our personalities. Our society is based on lending a helping hand to make everyone's journey through life a little easier.

When you reach out to give others a helping hand, whether great or small, the love and support you provide to care for others displays generosity, kindness and compassion. The world community needs to demonstrate these qualities more often and its love for people generally, especially through the turbulence caused by so many natural disasters occurring around the world (devastating earthquakes and floods and even droughts).

The best portion of a good man's life – his little, nameless, un-remembered acts of KINDNESS & LOVE. — William Wordsworth

By giving your time in helping others who have been unfortunately affected by these catastrophic events and helping to rebuild their lives, we can unite for humanity in tough times. Whether by helping flood victims in carrying their remaining goods of properties to safer grounds or by providing them with warm clothes that you do not need or, even better yet, to temporarily welcome them into your home until they get themselves sorted. Not only you are making a small difference to someone's life, but also your kind gestures in lending a hand to them will always be appreciated, and you will have made a large impact on their lives. At the same time, this can create an unexpected friendship connection for the long term.

With a little humility and compassion in every one of us, you and I can make a tremendous difference to this world by lending our helping hands wherever they are required. Be open and freely give of your time to support and help others out. It is unfortunate today we do not see many people going out of their way to help one another. Most people are too consumed with their busy lives to even be aware enough to recognise others around them, let alone see others in need of a helping hand.

Have you ever seen someone struggling to carry their groceries and just kept on walking by?

Why not offer to help them carry the bags and temporarily ease their burden a little? Even if it is a complete stranger, it is still another human being and they will appreciate the kind gesture. They may not have realised how heavy their load was until they picked it up. Now they are stuck carrying it and all they need is someone to come along who can lighten the load.

Lend a helping hand to guide and support an old woman or man on a walking stick to cross the road safely. Or simply when you see a mother struggling to push her pram up a hill or steps, kindly offer to help them. Any great or small kind gestures always benefit both people and connects them with love and gratitude. Don't you just love feeling good after seeing someone overcome their difficulties with your provision of help? Whether it is physical or verbal assistance? There are so many ways that you can help others and, in doing so, bring love into their lives as well as into yours.

So many people in our world face back-breaking physical, emotional and mental loads that are too overwhelming for them to endure on their own. They desperately need someone to reach out their hand, but they are usually too proud to ask for it. Whether it is helping someone carry heavy grocery bags, holding the door open for them or just offering them a shoulder to lean on, it is important that we extend our help to those who are in need around us.

Helping others is an easy way to give love back to the world. Another way that you can give love is by offering assistance when you know someone is struggling with an extra heavy workload. Maybe it is a special assignment at work or they have a big home repair project. As long as it doesn't interfere with your own responsibility and productivity, then it is great way to help someone while promoting teamwork and positive energy. Two people can usually get the job done faster than one, and they will appreciate that you offered to help. That person will also more likely be willing to offer you the same courtesy when your own workload becomes too much for you to handle.

It is always better to give than to receive!

You can also lend a helping hand by volunteering to help with fundraisers or charity events. Maybe the company you work for is organising a can drive and they need people to manage it. Maybe it is a local fun run to raise money for a good cause that is looking for someone to register the participants. If you are not someone who wants to run in the event, you can at least help with the behind the scenes planning.

If you can't feed a hundred people, then feed just one. ~Mother Teresa

It is the little things that we do in life that can have the greatest impact on the world around us. Maybe you see someone who looks rushed or panicked, so you let them cut in front of you in line at your local supermarket. Acknowledging them and showing concern for their time is a selfless way you can positively affect someone else's day. Saving someone a matter of minutes might ease their burden a little, but showing that you care enough to extend the courtesy could change their outlook altogether. Things can have very little impact on your own life, but the ripple effect that they cause can be priceless to someone else.

If you happen to have more money than you have time, then financial gifts are also a way to provide a helping hand to someone else in need. It really does not matter how you to choose to help someone else, as long as you are willing to help when you witness someone struggle to survive. You never know when the situation will be reversed and you will have to rely on the kindness of strangers.

Like everything in life, when you go out of your way to help another with good intentions, effectively you will generate an inbound flow of good karma in return. As long the intention is purely driven from the heart, your actions out of love and kindness can be felt and seen by the other's appreciative response. Go and live a more fulfilled life by giving others more of yourself by lending a helping hand to as many people as you can or whenever the opportunity arises. To demonstrate and share more love in this world

with your smallest kindnesses and caring actions, speaks high volumes for all to make a BIG difference to others and your life.

It does not make a difference how or why you choose to lend a helping hand, as long as you are making a conscience effort to think about the happiness of someone other than yourself. We are not alone in this world, and the more that we do to help one other, the more likely people will be there to help us when we need it. You are going to need help at some point in your life. So why not lend a helping hand the next time you see someone struggling and make a new friend in the process. They will appreciate your kindness and you will feel good about having a positive effect on someone else's life.

12.   Make Peace with Your Life

Sometimes, you might be going through painful personal experiences that have traumatically affected your well-being, so that your physical, mental and spiritual self all feel as though they are in ruins. I know I have encountered such turmoil feelings from my first relationship and, even today, I find this ordeal very hard to reflect on. The person that you once used to be has perished and the unknown self is questioning: 'Who is this person?' You might feel that you are losing your mind and are going 'crazy'. When nothing seems rational, sensible or logical right. Everything seems to be out of your control and you are unable to deal with your surroundings and the people in your life. You are close to the brink of madness with the emptiness feeling of nothingness! A soulless and an unemotional person in depths of despair.

I know this might be a lot for you to relate to, but it is precisely what I went through during some rough stages of my life. You probably think 'phew', wiping your brow, thinking your experience isn't that bad after all?! But then again, you might have lost a loved one and can completely comprehend where I am coming from. At times like this I recall, that all I needed to turn to find help was to pray within, seeking God to help me get me through my days and guide me out of my deep pain, personal problems and miseries.

Learning to contemplate internally, to find inner peace and a sense of oneness was my only strength. It allowed me to continue living without insanity or the loss of my 'soul'. Being in silence with nature and speaking of gratitude were my ways to find guidance and answers to my stresses and woes. Since then, I have now found myself again, and want to live my life in completeness, with the victory of love and gratitude, which I am happy to proclaim are part and parcel of my significant life experiences and the internal journey to find myself that has brought me here writing this book.

I am sure there have been moments in your life that you are not proud to admit to or that you would prefer to forget. Even if you are not happy with what has happened in your past, it should not have a negative impact on how you choose to live your life today. It is important that you make peace with your past, by learning what you can from each experience and then moving forward with a clear conscience.

Start by forgiving other people for things that they may have done to hurt you and also by forgiving yourself for any intentional or unintentional sins against others. Then take some quiet time to assess why you may have sinned and how you can avoid the same poor judgement call in the future. We all make mistakes and making peace with your life involves accepting that you cannot change what has already happened and instead you need to refocus your energy on the present and your future.

Acceptance with forgiveness follows the impediment of grief, allows you to embrace the measure of love within and to be able to love others' wrong doing forgivingly. Basically, to really forgive, you need to arrive at a self-loving state as in order to love that person enough to let go of all that's happened and the pain and suffering they have caused. In the process of healing yourself, you are making peace within, which is also learning to forgive yourself and giving yourself permission to move on with your life without any guilt or remnants of pain and sufferings.

> *To forgive is the highest, most beautiful form of love. In return, you will receive untold peace and happiness. — Robert Muller*

To forgive is the greatest feeling of love and joy one can experience. All of the grief and pain burdening your soul are finally released from your heart and mind, uplifting your sense of freedom and giving and sharing love and happiness for others to receive.

A great way to make peace with your life is to find a quiet spot when you can reflect on who you are and then take stock of all the positive views and what has happened to your life so far. Think about the areas that you need to work on and how you can improve on your current lifestyle choices. Anytime you are working on your own self-discovery, it is important that review both the good and the bad aspects of your personality.

If you only assess your flaws, you will end up feeling bad about yourself. Beating yourself up is never productive and it will not help you on your journey to abundant happiness. Every person has good qualities. There are special, unique attributes that you have that you should be proud of. Focus on the good within your spirit during your journey of self-discovery, so that you have a balanced perspective of your life.

When you make peace with where you have been in life, you will be more prepared for the path that lies ahead of you. You cannot turn back the clock and right your wrongs. There was a reason that things went wrong and the lessons that you learnt along the way have helped to shape who you are today. It is important that you remember that everything happens for a reason, whether good or bad. Optimistically, the reasons are mostly good and help to create a greater outlook and better outcomes to celebrate life. Appreciation of any good turn of events will increase your sense of internal awareness of happiness, thus, generating more continued goodness to circulate freely into your life.

13.   Take Care of Your Body

To have a healthy mind, body and soul is to nurture and love your overall well-being. A balance in life with regular exercise, a daily healthy diet, a regular silent time with nature or meditation... and keep on smiling! All of which are best viewed as ways of de-stressing in your busy life. Be in love with your physique and body. Take time to care for your body's requirements, internally and externally. Listen to what your body is intuitively telling you if you are deprived of certain nutrition or are suffering with aches and pains by not attending to your body's needs.

My exercise routine is regularly performed at least six days of the week, by walking and jogging, and sometimes practicing yoga. This might be too much for you to incorporate, but you can always adjust according to how many times in the day you can or want to exercise, as long as it is a regular routine. It all depends on your lifestyle. You may want to choose a particular style of exercising, perhaps going to the gym, playing team sports, doing yoga or Pilates etc., but always incorporate an aerobic form of exercise where possible to look after your cardiovascular system and blood flow to the heart.

I love to keep fit and be proactive. So, exercising for me is always easy to do and helps me to clear my mind and de-stress when I have a lot going on in my life. Regardless of the weather, rain or shine I still exercise! Plus, I love being out in the rain, so refreshing and cleansing!

With exercising, you get medical and health benefits with the release of endorphins ('happy' hormones) and even oxytocins ('love' hormones). An increase of your cardio (with aerobic stop and start jogging), helps your respiratory system, blood flow to the heart and circulation. On the plus side of regular exercising, your body's cells tend to repair themselves faster than the norm, helping you to keep young and in shape! According to health and scientific research, regular exercising helps to extend a human's life by 5 or 10 years. So get out there and start living a longer and healthier life by frequently exercising!

When you exercise, you need to replenish your energy with a daily healthy eating plan. My healthy eating usually consists of regular intakes of fresh salads, rice (brown), nuts and oats, eggs and occasionally fish, chicken or meat, as well as plenty of fresh fruit and vegies. It is important to drink plenty of water of course! At least eight glasses a day to get rid of the toxins in your body. And I always enjoy a daily dose of high antioxidant green tea. It is always good to feed your body with the most nutritious and healthy foods, such as 'super foods' (foods with high health benefits, e.g. antioxidants and foods that prevent diseases). You can research this on the internet.

Needless to say, you cannot go without indulging your tastebuds with other 'pleasurable' or 'bad' foods now and then. To maintain moderation in everything in life, at least once or twice a week I like to indulge in chocolate (preferably dark, which is high in antioxidants), chocolate cookies or triple choc chip muffins, chips etc... Yep, you name it, I love my chocolate! You get the idea of these foods — very yummy and tasty but not good for your body. So less of this is best.

Sometimes in your busy life, you need to replenish your soul, to have some quiet time to yourself and to just be in the present moment. This is a superb way to also de-stress and be in touch with nature and your immediate surroundings. I find this is the best time, where I can be in 'oneness' with nature and the appreciation of mother earth's creation. Also, it is a time for me to be at peace and feel calmness, or give prayers of gratitude. I do this before my exercise, when walking and jogging, or in-between my breaks. Try this if you have not yet added it into your daily or weekly life. You will feel much more energised with a whole sense of self.

Meditation is also a great way to de-stress and be centred with your one-self. I thoroughly enjoy meditation as it helps me to clear my mind and have inner peace. Or, sometimes, if I have questions needing answers, I use meditation as a way to connect with my higher source or the higher 'intelligence' to help in clarifying my needs. I always feel incredibly relaxed and vibrationally charged coming out of a meditation.

Nurture your mind with meditation to cultivate a greater sense of inner peace and love, and a healthy, clear consciousness. Incorporate meditation into your daily routine, 10, 15 to 30 minutes with music or without, either in the morning after waking up or before going to sleep. This will help you to change how you feel about the day ahead or to be more relaxed for bed. Recommended healing meditation music for internal peace and bliss to ease the mind: http://tinyurl.com/mfc7jzn.

Always have a beaming smile on your face, it is the best way to uplift your mood and start your day with a positive direction. Of course, do not force or fake your smile, as it is should be genuinely felt within.

Smiling and laughing naturally makes you feel good or even amazingly great, with the release of more happy hormones of endorphins throughout your body. Not only you are in a happy state but a bright smile is pleasant for others approaching to welcome you with a smile in return. Bring plenty of love towards yourself and give it out to others. Smile often, show your sparkle for everyone to enjoy, and spread happiness, including towards yourself!

Remember that your body is a temple and it is important to your happiness that you respect it and treat it well. You are only given one vessel to experience this world in and you should want that vessel to be in the best condition possible. You should be willing to put the work into it, so that you can be proud of the results! Part of loving yourself involves making the time to properly take care of your body.

Everyone needs exercise and a healthy diet to maintain their optimal health. Our bodies are fragile and easily susceptible to disease and illness when we do not give them the nutrients to survive. By choosing foods that are rich in nutrients and vitamins, we can ensure our body has what it needs to perform at its best.

Exercise is essential to your health and happiness, plus it can be a lot of fun. There are so many ways that you can get in a workout while spending time with the people who matter. You can organise a baseball, basketball or football game with your family or friends. You can also plan a walk or a hike where you can appreciate nature at the same time.

A more physically fit body will also help with your confidence and self-esteem. When you are in good shape, you feel better about yourself and you are more willing to challenge yourself physically. Maintaining better internal and external health will also give you more power to do what you want with your life, instead of being limited by excess weight or poor physical conditioning.

You are only given one body and, out of respect for it, it is crucial that you keep it in the best condition possible. Everything in life comes down to making good choices, which includes your health and fitness. Choose to care about your body and your body will be in the right condition to care for you. Also, the better that you treat your body, the longer it will last.

14.   Give Inspiration

Be an inspiration to others by inspiring and motivating them to help them reach their goals. Deep inside of each and every one of us, we all have what it takes to inspire others with our tools, talents and life experiences or knowledge. Even without it, you might be unknowingly inspiring someone today. For instance, your positive outlook on everything you do and life in general. You might be passionate about a hobby or writing, or fulfilling your goals and, when people see this side of you, they are encouraged and feel they can do the same and change their lives.

By giving others inspirations, you are essentially giving the love of who you are for them to be inspired by, or acting as their role model. Unintentionally, you might be constantly speaking with positive encouragements to whomever you may come across. And no, I am not talking about lecturing others either — only an understanding conversation with positive solutions and encouragement. You may not realise just what happened until that person thanks you for the positive helpful advice you just gave to them.

The gratitude in that person's response will help you to realise how much love and care you have just given to them. Hence, when you give yourself to be an inspiration to someone or others, the love and gratitude are always exchanged between you.

It is very rewarding to feel and see others' body language and emotions divert to an uplifting positive change so that they become full of drive, determination and willing to make changes to their lives. In fact, they already knew to identify their problems and all that time had the solutions inside them, but had failed to recognise this, until someone provided them with a little reinforcing encouragement. This is really a work of inspiration! See how easy it is to help others just by being a good listener and having a positive outlook in every situation?!

There is no gift more rewarding than giving inspiration to someone in desperate need of it. I was at a particularly low point in my life and a friend inspired me to make some pretty big changes. I was unhappy with my body weight, unhappy with my career and my self-esteem was at an all-time low. She had just completed her first marathon and I was envious of her success as I watched her beam with pride. I wanted that feeling for myself.

I shared my thoughts with her and she immediately encouraged me. She was also kind enough to offer help with my training, which I desperately needed. I started by only committing to walk a half marathon, which was a feat in itself for a 20 lb (9.07 kg), overweight unhealthy eater, and I paid my registration before my self-doubt had a chance to change my mind. After I felt the incredible boost from crossing that finish line, I inspired myself to start eating healthier and I started running.

The amazing self-esteem boost that overwhelmed my mind the second I crossed the finish line was a feeling that was indescribably self-rewarding and liberating. All of a sudden, I felt that with hard work and determination I could accomplish anything that I wanted to do. Later that year I left my stable, yet unrewarding job to chase my dream career. Unimaginable success has followed me ever since, which is why I choose to inspire others.

If your actions inspire others to dream more, learn more, do more and become more, you are a leader. — *John Quincy Adams*

Since I was inspired by someone else, I try to do everything in my power to inspire anyone who is seeking it. I post motivational quotes on Facebook and Twitter, along with comments about recent feats that I have overcome. It is always good to keep yourself fully inspired every day with inspirational written quote cards, either from yourself or from those you are inspired by. Examples of provokingly, powerful and inspirational thoughts cards include: http://tinyurl.com/ksqvpg2.

As you can see throughout this book are some of my most valued and loved inspirational quotes containing profound insights and teachings, to help you to understand the powerful words and of the morals. I also make sure to always acknowledge and sincerely praise other people's accomplishments. It is important to get just as excited about someone else's good fortune as we do about our own.

Several times throughout the past few years, people that I only know as acquaintances have contacted me and thanked me for the inspiration. I had no idea that my positive attitude and self-help journey had motivate changes and improvements in other people's lives. Their letters of appreciation inspire me to keep pushing forward on my mission of self-improvement and in continuing to help others to make a difference and to change their lives by helping them to activate their inner love and gratitude. I inspire them and they inspire me to continue to give inspiration.

Whether great or small, be an inspiration to one or many others, have a room full of attentive listeners ready to be inspired by your knowledge and life experiences. You can help them bring positive growth and self-empowerment into their lives. Don't you get really inspired when you hear someone talk on stage or when you are at seminars? The speaker's positive attitude to 'Yes you can achieve anything in life!' is effective and contagiously inspirational. So go out there and share what you have to give and be an inspiration to others! Every inspiration to another makes a positive impact to change our own and other's lives, creating an inspirational world of real purpose.

I am so thankful for my year five primary teacher Mr Carroll whom had appraised of me that I would be a great author some day in the future — which, at that time, I did not think much about. Until now, his words and belief in me have inspired me to live up to those memorable words of encouragement to be truly living my dream life in reality.

15. Create Gratitude Moments

Sharing your love with your family, friends and even acquaintances in every special moment are what truly define what to consider precious and to be most grateful for. These gratitude moments are times of celebrations, in any form of gatherings such as birthdays, anniversaries, weddings, bbqs, picnics, camping, coffee or drinking with friends, or any excuse to have a gathering of some sort.

These are special moments, where you can experience precious time with your loved ones and enjoy each other's presence. Moments like these are not replaceable and should be cherished by all. One way is to take pictures or videos of memorable times spent with your loved ones. It is important to always be grateful for these moments, treasure them in your memory and share with others in the future.

When you are sharing your time, love and gratitude in special moments with others, you are creating a living moment of real-time happiness.'
— *Natasha Dao*

When everyone gathers together there are always moments of joy and laughter to be shared. An ambience of warm, loving connection with others brings a sense of 'liveliness' to our own awakening and in experiencing living in the moment.

Can you recall the last time you spent a memorable moment like this, which you are most grateful for? I certainly can and really love going to any and every event that I have the opportunity to attend. My recent (at the time of writing this book), and greatest gratitude moments would have to be spending every precious moment that I can with a very special person that I deeply care about.

We were in the early stage of developing a beautiful, loving and romantic relationship. Unfortunately, he was in the transition stage of moving to another state for his career. So I made every moment that I had with him special by sharing loving gratitude times together before he left. These moments are very special to me and I will always hold them close in memory, to appreciate the times that we shared. The last thing I want is to regret that I did not spend enough time, but to be grateful for the moments we experienced which I will always cherish in my heart.

Gratitude moments are those memorable experiences that naturally occur when family and friends are celebrating a special moment in someone's life. The greatest life experiences can be found any time people who really care about each other are gathered together in celebration. You can be the one to initiate the event by offering to host a party or put together a family dinner. It does not even need to be a special occasion. Sometimes it is just nice to get together and you can celebrate the fact that you are grateful that you have each other.

Gratitude for the present moment and the fullness of life now is the true prosperity. — Eckhart Tolle

If you do not have time for all of the work that comes with hosting a gratitude moment or celebration, please make sure that you take the time to attend when you are invited to one. You should never use work commitments as an excuse to miss out on a holiday, birthday or anniversary parties.

It is important that you recognise the significance of these milestones in your own life and the lives of the people who matter to you. Wedding anniversaries should be a celebration of many years of marital bliss with someone whom you love dearly. Birthdays are a sign that another year has passed in someone's journey and they should feel excitement for the upcoming year. These days are special for a reason.

Another way you can create a gratitude moment is by gathering people with similar interests together for a think tank or an informal chat. Usually, when you unite positive, influential voices together it will result in incredible ideas, innovation and inspiration. Try to plan something fun and exciting that everyone can participate in. Here is another idea to form a group together online and offline, and in sharing memorable, yet fun and learning and meeting with others: http://www.meetup.com.

If the group you are gathering is athletic, you can also organise a sporting event, outdoor excursion or a nature hike. Working out together can bring people close together while also allowing you the opportunity to get to know each other better.

Make sure that you are not excluding anyone who should be a part of your gratitude celebration. Holidays and parties are about bringing together everyone, regardless of their differences to rejoice happily as a group. If you intentionally or unintentionally leave somebody out of the experience, it may make them feel unwanted or unloved. Nothing can be gained from making another human being feel unloved.

When we give cheerfully and accept gratefully, everyone is blessed.
— *Maya Angelou*

Gratitude moments can happen at a backyard barbeque, a family reunion or even a company picnic. The important thing is that you get involved and that you make sure that you take the time to enjoy conversing with those around you. Work is never a good excuse to miss a gratitude moment. There will always be opportunities to work on building your fortune, but true happiness will not be found until you spend time building your relationships.

If you waste too much time working on you career and personal advancement while neglecting the people who matter, they may not be there when you finally find the time for them. Stay connected with the people you love by making sure that you actively participate in every celebration and special occasion. You will strengthen your relationships and most likely have a lot of fun at the same time.

16. Give Forgiveness

Life is too short to hold grudges when someone has unintentionally or even intentionally hurt you. Vengeance, anger or retaliation is never the answer. Unfortunately, for some people, there are things that simply cannot be forgotten no matter how much time has passed. There are wrongs that have been committed that are indescribably painful, but forgiveness is still necessary in order for you to move on. It doesn't mean that you should be reunited with a past abuser, but you need to let go of the pain and forgive them for their sin against you.

The weak can never forgive. Forgiveness is the attribute of the strong.
— *Mahatma Gandhi*

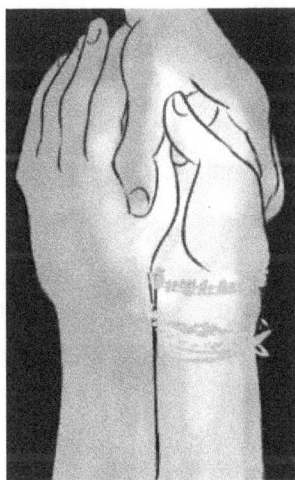

For some, forgiving is intolerable and excruciatingly painful because the wounds of the past are so deep. You can hide your feelings and not think that you even care about it all, but in fact, you are really suppressing your emotions and the associated pain. It hurts even more when you are trying to let go of the pains of the heart. You can try to forget the past and what happened by disregarding situation and what another person has done, forcing yourself to bury it all so you can move on with your life.

When you find yourself feeling a sense of loss or grief or even heartbreak, especially when the other person has played a significant part of your life, you are left with a sense of internal 'emptiness' and you see yourself as being an unloved soul. I know this may sound strange, but that was the experience I had gone through and had felt. It was as though there were some deep unresolved issues that were constantly and consciously burdening my mind and soul. Something was weighing me down terribly, affecting every part of my body and sub-consciousness.

Ironically, you feel such pain that you are reminded of that person each and every day, even though you think you have moved on. You recall flashes of anger and resentment that strike at your hurt, and the painful memories return again. There will be times when you will feel yourself less loved and unworthy, and you will cry for sympathy. Strangely, you will also see the 'goodness' or love of the person who has done wrong by you, for this implies you are truly ready to forgive the other person.

To get through your 'grieving' process, you need to reconcile with the other person in your heart and be able to give them absolute love and forgiveness in order to achieve closure. Importantly, start by giving love to yourself as much as you would to that person. Allowing yourself to open your heart unconditionally in healing and abandonment of all wounds inflicted by past pain. When you do this, you are facing them with no or little remaining hurt.

If there is still pain between the two of you, an understanding of what that pain is and why you are feeling it needs open expression in a nurturing discussion — but without rehashing past details and events. Of course, this will work only if the other person is understanding enough to cooperate and also ready to find closure themselves. After an exchange of loving understanding for one another, both can conclude with expressions such as 'I love you and I forgive you'.

These profound words are powerful tokens of forgiveness and acceptance, all through the defiant meaning of LOVE. So, forgiving for others creates healing and forgiveness for yourself. You can forgive and not forget, but to need to accept the past with forgiving love.

Don't let past wrongs dictate your future!

> *Forgiveness is more than just a verbal response when someone apologises. It has to be felt within and come from a place of peace and acceptance. Everyone has done something wrong at one point or another during the course of their life and, although it does not excuse their behaviour, they are only human. They can easily fall victim to temptation or evil without realising the pain their actions are causing. Forgiving others is in the healing of forgiving oneself.* — Natasha Dao

If someone is honestly regretful and they have made an attempt to remedy the situation, then you should offer your forgiveness without any strings attached. That does not mean that you should tolerate it if they hurt you again, but if they have truly changed their ways, then it is best to forgive, forget and move on. You will not gain anything by burying yourself with thoughts of revenge or animosity towards them.

There is something incredibly powerful that comes with giving forgiveness to someone who has treated you poorly. It gives you the control of your life back and it allows you to accept what has happened and move forward with a clear conscience. You are the one choosing how to respond instead of allowing them to force a reaction. When you can let go of the past, you can reshape your future.

17.   You Are Not Alone!

Often times when we are feeling at our most vulnerable, we keep our feelings buried inside and cut ourselves off from the people who care about us the most. We do not want to admit to the fact that we are struggling, so instead we try to deal with problems completely on our own.

You are not alone!

There are always people you can turn to who are willing to help you through the rough patches that are an inevitable fact of life. Whether it is your family, your friends or a local outreach program, there are people out there who care about you and who want to see you happy.

There is no shame in admitting that you need help. Let go of your pride and allow others to support you wherever you need it most. Asking for help from others is not to say you are weak in any way, but you are realising your own strengths by seeking the support of others. Life is not easy and that is why it was not meant to be lived as a solo mission. Sometimes it is easy just to keep yourself busy doing what you love, not needing anyone else.

That is easily done by when we want to accomplish something, get things done or need to reach our goals. Don't you admit this is the case? Or, unless I can see that person or others can give me good reasons to speed up the process and help me to reach my goals faster.

From my personal perspective, I am the type of person who, when a task does not really require others, I am happy to do everything myself. When I am focusing on my goals or on a target, I tend to block out all interruptions and even my surroundings! Just like when I am writing this book. All I have playing in the background is easy listening music and off I go in the zone of writing!

I know this may be extreme, but that is just how I work as a person. Needless to say, if I feel I am stressed in some ways, either related to my book or personal life, I will resort to others or my friends for help and confide in them for moral support and love. So do not reserve yourself, let others help you out. As humans, we can only bond through the love of one another and helping each other.

I am sure there have been times when someone else has leaned on you for support and it is only fair that you can in return lean on them or someone else when your own burden becomes too heavy to bear by yourself. Giving each other a helping hand is a natural instinct that says we are nurturing enough to show love and care for others. When you are offered help or give help to others, always accept with appreciation and gratitude for good intentions. It really and truly goes both ways.

It is important that you make strong connections with the people in your life, so you feel comfortable turning to them when you need help or advice. That is why having only give and take relationships is so vital to your overall happiness. Not only are you are strengthening your love with others so you can rely on them when you need their support, but also you are building a strong long-term bond of communication and mutual trust with others. A grateful and loving friendship will always last and see each other through the tough times!

Sometimes professional help or guidance may be needed and there is absolutely nothing wrong with it. There is an old stigma that talking to a counsellor or psychiatrist is a sign of weakness, but it is a really great option when all you need is someone to talk to about your concerns. They are experienced at handling problems just like yours and they do it every day. It is actually a sign of strength and maturity to admit that you cannot fix things on your own. Always good to allow a third party to interject their thoughts, ideas and advices in helping you and your problems to get sorted professionally.

It does not really matter if you turn to your best friend, your mum, favourite aunt or a psychiatrist, as long as you go to someone who is willing to help you through your problems. You are not alone in this world and there is always someone willing to help when you need it the most. Always reach out to others when you need help, whether the problem is great or small, you are in difficult times or not, for others will openly reach out to you to give their love and support in return.

Seek seldom in others, helping and nurturing our love and support for one kind. — Natasha Dao

18.   Give Respect

Happiness will come from learning how to give sincere respect to others and then demanding the same in return. It all comes down to the golden rule that we should treat people the way that we want to be treated. If you show people respect for their opinions, respect for their efforts and respect for their right to live their life the way they want to live it, then in due course they will show you the same respect.

Treat others as you would have done unto yourself. — *Natasha Dao*

It's ironic that some will tend to demand or request respect from others constantly throughout their lives, when they do not have the slightest understanding of what these words really mean, or an insight and inner perspective or understanding of not respecting themselves, yet they seek respect from others. Not only are they ungrateful people but they expect or think that they deserve respect as though it is due to them.

You have probably encountered these sorts of people every day in your work place or on the streets and in the super market — you know who I am talking about?! These people usually have an ego issue and think they are superior to others, especially when there is an hierarchical order in place. There is nothing that can be done with these types of people. All you can do is to let them be, for they have their own issues to sort out within themselves in the course of their own life.

If you do not respect others, you are implying that you do not respect yourself, and if you expect or demand respect, you are obviously not going to get that respect in return! This is all a reflection of yourself that is mirrored and projected into your outer world. Your perception of who you are, your values, your self-worth, your integrity and your actions are all composites of your true self-love and respect as a whole person.

Others will see this in you and will either repulse you or offer you their respect. But remember to at least give each and every people the respect and love that they deserve as humans. You and I deserve to be loved, so give others the same respect, regardless of whether you like who they are as a person, how they behave and act, or that they have nothing in common with you. Just respect others simply for who they are with unconditional love.

Everyone is different and that is what makes our lives so incredibly special. Part of finding happiness in this crazy world is learning how to respect people's differences and appreciate them for their unique perspective on life. They may not share the same religious beliefs, but it does not mean they do not share the same core values. Always give others the benefit of the doubt without any form of judgment. It really all comes down to respecting each other's differences, but in the end we all share a common desire: to love and be loved in unity.

Giving and showing your respect to another is an acknowledgement of your appreciation for who they are as a person, and not about what they do or have achieved. It is not their credentials or their powerful position which ultimately gives them the right or a reason to be respected. It is unfortunate that we see this in many current events and in people who shape the world in which we live today; for example, political figures, big conglomerates and organisations, workplace authorities and the alike.

I am not saying that they do not deserve to be respected, but only for real and genuine reasons, not because others favour and praise them for their charisma, popularity or trendy image. You should not just follow the crowd and give that same respect to them. Know in yourself to respect others with true conviction from love and appreciation and nothing else. If we all applied this in our lives, our world would be a place of respectful citizens, from young to old, fat or skinny, black or white skin, small corporate and empowered big companies, all working together to be appreciated and loved as equal individuals and respected entities.

It is also important that you show respect to your elders. The older generations have experienced more in their lives and they have wisdom that they can share with you. By choosing to show them respect and taking a personal interest in the incredible lives that they have lived, your elders may teach you their own tips and tricks on how to live a happier life.

It is also important that you respect your co-workers, customers, employers and anyone that you need to interact with on a daily basis. It will be easier to enjoy your professional life, if you have positive and constructive relationships. People will treat you better when there is a mutual respect for one another. If you are willing to give respect, you will most likely receive their respect in return.

19.   Open Your Heart

There is nothing more beautiful than the state of feeling blissful love when you are ready to experience it with an open heart, especially to give and receive love with someone special. When you are purely committed to give all that you are, and how you feel about that person, your love can be measured by the actions that come from your heart. To be compassionate from a very loving space, you and your partner must be open enough to trust and support each other in every possible way.

Giving all your time and effort to be with each other is truly gratifying and feels timeless when you are in each other's presence. The passing of time does not mean a thing as, when you are together, time does not really matter and tends to fly. In fact, nothing really matters but yourself and the shared love of your partner. Both are completely lost in time but not lost in love.

In the time of writing this book, my experience in an endearing and loving relationship, I would claim to say is purely driven from the compassionate heart... a true love. Knowing that you care so much for each other and the other person's well-being when you are not with them makes it even harder for you to concentrate on other parts of your life.

When you open yourself to give and receive love, unconditionally and honestly, you are allowing yourself to draw in love from others who also value and appreciate the same. Do not hesitate to give your love wholeheartedly with an open mind to experience a fulfilling and grateful lifetime love. Otherwise, you will not know what you are missing out on in life. Everyone deserves to be in love with the right person or their soul mate.

Loving from an open heart brings great joy and happiness to yourself and to others in the appreciation of your life. It attracts more abundance, finance, opportunities and like-minded people. To be coming from a compassionate loving self, you are embracing all parts of who you are, and sharing with an acceptance of each other's faults and traits.

The odds are that you have had your heart broken at some point in your life. It may be the betrayal of a lover, a friend who broke your trust or a parent who let you down. Regardless of how you were hurt, it forces most people to build up their defence system. They want to avoid being hurt again, so they build a wall around themselves.

> *Breathe. Let go. And remind yourself that this very moment is the only one you know you have for sure.* — Oprah Winfrey

The older we get, the more often we are hurt and the less likely we are to put our trust in someone new. We think we are doing ourselves a favour by placing guards around our heart, but in actuality, we are blocking real love from entering. We need to have faith that someone sincerely loves us for who we are instead of depriving ourselves of the job of being unconditionally loved.

Only in believing and loving yourself completely will you build an inner faith and strength, and rediscover what love can bring into your life. You must be willingly to give it a try. Do not be afraid of failing a relationship, for without failures in your life you would not learn from your experiences, or grow as a better person each and every day. In general, you need to take risks in life —some will be educated and calculated risks. But one way or another, we live and breathe to make certain risks. In this case, it is called 'a leap of faith'. Or, more nicely put, it is listening from your intuition to what your heart is telling you to do. You cannot go wrong when you are following your heart.

There is no greater love than when two people rely on each other, encourage each other and fully believe in one another. That means accepting that the other person is not perfect and that you love all of their attributes and all of their flaws. If you want someone to care about you in good times and bad, then it is important that you are able to offer the same to them.

LOVE is the only reality and it is not a mere sentiment. It is the ultimate truth that lies at the HEART of CREATION.— Rabindranath Tagore

By opening your heart to the possibilities of true love, you will find love in every relationship. You may love the way the cashier at the grocery story greets you with a smile, you may love that your neighbour cuts your grass without you knowing it, or you may love the fact that a sibling calls you every week to see how you are doing. Any meaningful exchange can be viewed with loving eyes when you start with an open heart.

Not only you will be more appreciative of every person that comes into your life, but you will love others from a compassionate place, with no pre-conceived expectations or judgements. You will see them from the heart with an unbiased love. In opening your heart, naturally, your love will expand to greater heights in everything you see, do and personally experience. For example, witnessing the vibrantly beautiful colours of the flowers in your garden or at the park, even though you had not noticed them from before, or in marvelling at the sunrise or sunset that you have taken for granted every day with appreciation and love.

The trick to opening your heart is focusing on the good relationships and the special moments you have had throughout your life. If you are not willing to allow those people and experiences into your life, you would have missed out on some of your happiest memories.

It is better to have loved and lost, than to have never loved at all!

Even when a good relationship has ended badly, there are still many great moments that you were fortunate enough to have shared together during the good times. The last memory may be tragic, but they could not have all been bad days together. There was a reason that person meant something to you, otherwise you would not be as hurt about the relationship failing. Try to think about all of the good times that you shared and how those memories have shaped the rest of your life.

Would your life be any better if you hadn't met that person at all?

Hopefully, the honest answer is no. There were reasons why certain people came into your life and, regardless of whether they are there now, they were an important part of your growth and development. Each relationship has its unique qualities and you would be a different person if you had never had it.

So, why shouldn't you be willing to open your heart to a new relationship? Who knows what exciting and life-changing events might happen if you make the decision to give somebody else a try. Maybe it will last forever or it could end up in disaster, but if you never take the chance, you will always wonder what could have been. Just be willing to open your heart and allow what is meant to be to happen.

20.   Give Life 100% of Your Effort

Your life is a gift and it should never be wasted or taken for granted. Live your life 100% with every ounce of breath and enthusiasm, put in the time and effort to become your higher potential self. Every day you should ask yourself what you can honestly do to improve your own life and what you can do to improve the lives of those around you. How are you to serve others and get paid for doing what you love? Am I happy and fulfilled in my current career? Sometimes it is good to reflect on these questions to gain insight into whether you are really living at your uttermost true self and purpose.

Throughout our lives, we all go through many transitions of changes in jobs and careers. But whether we are truly living according to our highest values, our highest potential self should leave us happy doing what we love most every day. Some people love to make a big difference in their lives so they can make a big difference for others, in creating businesses or charities or even in writing books, while others are happy to be the best parents to their children. Whatever the case may be, just make sure it is your highest priority in life, giving you the greatest internal fulfilment of love and happiness for the life you want.

Simply, whatever you choose to do in your life, make the most out of your greatest intention to love and live the life that you deserve. Follow what your heart desires and never fall short on settling to just live comfortably or to get by. Live inspiringly for yourself and for others with excellence! Do not be ordinary, be EXTRA ordinary!

We all have what it takes and all deserve to create the life that we choose; to live abundantly, spiritually and inspiringly. You can have anything in your life according to your heart's desire, having the dream job that you have always wanted to obtain or create, and having the soulful, understanding and trusting relationship with that right loving partner or soul mate, or having the ideal loving and nurturing family and friends. Anything is possible really, when you set your mind to make it happen!

Do not let society or your family dictate what job or career you should have, who you should marry or be with, and how you should live or be like everyone else. It saddens me to see so many people living their lives with self-dissatisfaction and who are unhappy. Knowing what they do best, but feeling that their overall life is not what they intended and that it is somehow incomplete. There is much more to life than mediocrity.

Do you resonate with this? Are you living the life that you should be? Going with my inner calling or my heart's desire, I left my career a long time ago. I did not know what I was going to do, but I knew for sure that I was destined for a much bigger life than what I was doing in my former job. I am very blessed to be finally on the road to achieving my real purpose — living my life as an author, entrepreneur and philanthropist.

There are so many endeavours that I would love to undertake, but for now, one step at a time, I am happy to pour all my energy towards being an international best-selling author with many more books to write. In helping to bring the message of this very important book, with the intention of self-empowerment and discovering the higher purpose to life, as well as bringing the healing and the activation of inner love and gratitude into many people's lives.

By helping to make a difference to the life journey of others, in gratitude, love, life and happiness and to live the life that they deserve, in awakening them to the right path to their goals and dreams. Bringing my first book and message out into the world will help me to move even closer to my ultimate life goal of being an abundant philanthropist helping to alleviate poverty and enriching many underprivileged children world-wide through my own company and future charity.

Be courageous, creative and inspiring to create the life that is fulfilling and purposeful, where every day you wake up with a feeling of motivation and are inspired to give all that you have in working towards the goals of your higher self. This is what I would call your dream job — what you are truly passionate about and love, to make all the difference on your journey of life. Have fun with it and be adventurous! Life is really what you want to make of it! I am sure many ideas will pop into your head, but the trick is following through on them. If you make a commitment to do something, then you should feel obligated to do it and follow through to the end.

Don't just talk about it, BE about it! Walk your talk!

You have the power to do anything that you want with your life, but you are going to have to work hard and stay focused on the end results if you expect to succeed. Your life deserves 100% of your efforts and if you give all of yourself to this life, an abundance of happiness is sure to follow.

21.   Say I Love You

The more you are motivated by LOVE, the more fearless and free your action will be.— Dalai Lama

Human love is strongly felt in the forms of physical closeness and affection through the embraces of hugs and kisses. This bond and loving connection is one that we all love to be associated with every day: sharing love with your lover, partner and family and friends, or even strangers and acquaintances; parents kissing and saying farewell to their children when departing for school in the morning; hugging someone when welcoming them back from a trip at the airport and letting them know how much you missed them; or a meet and greet with a kiss and hug at a close family and friends gathering.

Sometimes, it is not enough to show your love without expressing those three magical words, 'I love you'. In speaking from the heart, with deep emotion, these three words are highly important. They are a deep expression of love that one can only say to another openly, and intimately, such as in an intimate and romantic relationship when you open your heart fully to give all you have, and to receive unconditionally. The depth feelings from the expression of the words 'I love you' is powerful enough to open up the truthfulness and sincerity one can only see in vulnerability. You are creating a strong loving bond, a union of compassionate understanding and passionate feeling for one another in a beautiful, nurturing relationship.

It is unfortunate that in some relationships, couples are not open enough to express how they feel for each other, they are afraid of getting hurt so try to protect their heart wall from the pain. Their fear of rejection and of the other person not feeling the same love for them is sadly left unsaid with these three felt words. There should be no right or wrong time to say 'I love you' in an intimate loving relationship between two people, as long as you and your lover or partner feel the same loving connection, deeply rooted in each other's heart.

If you feel the need to express yourself and use those special words during the growth of a very loving relationship, then do not hesitate to pour out your heart about how you feel about the other person. If not they do not already, your partner will see this immense love for them through your actions and affectionate words. Give them a sweet text or a note to express those words that mean so much to you if you are unable to say them, or you feel it is too early in the development of the relationship. Let the other person know in one way or another how important they are to you and that the love you both share is very special.

Do not let your pride get in the way but permit yourself to freely and emotionally express your love with strong heart-felt words. Saying 'I Love You' should not be left as a means to test who should say it first. The last thing you want is to regret that you did not get to say 'I love you' to them when they are gone interstate, overseas or are no longer part of your life, you need to value and appreciate the love that was shared.

When two people are deeply in love, both hearts are equally opened to the giving and receiving of unconditional love. With such love, every heartbeat is in tune and shares an amazing, meaningful love on a spiritual and soul level.

One thing I have noticed as I have grown older is people seem to say 'I love you' less and less often. Such powerful words do not need to be reserved for only your significant other or your immediate family on special occasions and holidays. Saying 'I love you' is a great way to remind the people in your life that they matter and that someone truly cares about them. Any time you are sharing an intimate conversation, saying good bye or spending quality time together, you should conclude the exchange with the words, I love you!'

That way, the last memory both of you have together is the sharing your verbal commitment of love. Within time, you will have many more opportunities to show and say it again, but at least you know that the last time you spoke it ended with those three powerful words. It is so important that you make sure to tell people that you love them before it is too late. We are only blessed with a certain amount of time on this earth and if you wait too long to say what you feel it may be too late… so tell someone that you really care about them by using those three special words 'I love you' as your measure of immense appreciation and love for them.

Always tell someone how you feel because opportunities are lost in the blink of any eye, but regret can last forever. — Unknown

I am fortunate and blessed not to have lost someone close to me or have anyone pass away, without having the opportunity to tell them that I love and deeply care for them. But, by not taking every day for granted, I am always happily sharing my love with words and actions of kindness and saying at times 'I love you' to my loved ones, for every moment is preciously lived.

Whether it is with my lover and partner, close friends, mother or grandmother, every ounce of time spent together is an invaluable gift, to be sharing love with one another. I would not know how I would be able to cope if I did not get all the chances to show and express how much I love them either through kind gestures or with the special words 'I love you... and you can never say it enough. Be open to freely express wholeheartedly these profoundly touching words of 'I love you' whenever you get the opportunity to whom you care the most.

You can also use those incredible words to lift someone's spirits. If someone special is going through a tough time, verbally remind them that they are loved. You can show your love by appreciating their presence and in demonstrating personal kind actions, but some people need to hear the words in order to truly feel loved. Three simple words could be all that it takes to change someone else's outlook on life.

Next time you feel love inside, say it out loud! Share it and spread it to the people who matter, so they know how much they really mean to you. Verbal exchanges of love are a great channel for an abundance of love and an abundance of happiness.

Say *I Love You* in 100 different languages

English – I love you
Afrikaans – Ek het jou lief
Albanian – Te dua
Arabic – Ana behibak (to male)
Arabic – Ana behibek (to female)
Armenian – Yes kez sirumen
Bambara – M'bi fe
Bengali – Ami tomake bhalobashi
Belarusian – Ya tabe kahayu
Bisaya – Nahigugma ako kanimo
Bulgarian – Obicham te
Cambodian – Soro lahn nhee ah
Cantonese Chinese – Ngo oiy ney a
Catalan – T'estimo
Cherokee – Tsi ge yu i
Cheyenne – Ne mohotatse
Chichewa – Ndimakukonda
Corsican – Ti tengu caru (to male)
Creol – Mi aime jou
Croatian – Volim te
Czech – Miluji te
Danish – Jeg Elsker Dig
Dutch – Ik hou van jou
Elvish – Amin mela lle
(Lord of The Rings)
Esperanto – Mi amas vin
Estonian – Ma armastan sind
Ethiopian – Afgreki'
Faroese – Eg elski teg
Farsi – Doset daram
Filipino – Mahal kita
Finnish – Mina rakastan sinua
French – Je t'aime, Je t'adore
Frisian – Ik hâld fan dy
Gaelic – Ta gra agam ort
Georgian – Mikvarhar
German – Ich liebe dich
Greek – S'agapo
Gujarati – Hoo thunay prem karoo choo
Hiligaynon – Palangga ko ikaw
Hawaiian – Aloha Au Ia`oe
Hebrew (Thanks Lilach)
Hebrew to male: "ani ohev otcha"
(said by male) "Ohevet ot'cha"
(said by female)
Hebrew to female: "ani ohev otach"
(said by male) "ohevet Otach"
(said by female)
Hiligaynon – Guina higugma ko ikaw
Hindi – Hum Tumhe Pyar Karte hae
Hmong – Kuv hlub koj
Hopi – Nu' umi unangwa'ta
Hungarian – Szeretlek(Thanks D..ra!)
Icelandic – Eg elska tig
Ilonggo – Palangga ko ikaw
Indonesian – Saya cinta padamu
Inuit – Negligevapse
Irish – Taim i' ngra leat
Italian – Ti amo
Japanese – Aishiteru

Kannada – Naanu ninna preetisuttene
Kapampangan – Kaluguran daka
Kiswahili – Nakupenda
Konkani – Tu magel moga cho
Korean – Sarang Heyo
Latin – Te amo
Latvian – Es tevi miilu
Lebanese – Bahibak
Lithuanian – Tave myliu
Luxembourgeois – Ech hun dech g..er
Macedonian – Te Sakam
Malay – Saya cintakan mu / Aku cinta padamu
Malayalam – Njan Ninne Premikunnu
Maltese – Inhobbok
Mandarin Chinese – Wo ai ni
Marathi – Me tula prem karto
Mohawk – Kanbhik
Moroccan – Ana moajaba bik
Nahuatl – Ni mits neki
Navaho – Ayor anosh'ni
Norwegian – Jeg Elsker Deg
Pandacan – Syota na kita!!
Pangasinan – Inaru Taka
Papiamento – Mi ta stimabo
Persian – Doo-set daaram
Pig Latin – Iay ovlay ouyay
Polish – Kocham Ciebie
Portuguese – Eu te amo
Romanian – Te iubesc
Russian – Ya tebya liubliu
Scot Gaelic – Tha gra..dh agam ort
Serbian – Volim te
Setswana – Ke a go rata
Sign Language – ,..,/ (represents position of
fingers when signing'I Love You')
Sindhi – Maa tokhe pyar kendo ahyan
Sioux – Techihhila
Slovak – Lu`bim ta
Slovenian – Ljubim te
Spanish – Te quiero / Te amo
Swahili – Ninapenda wewe
Swedish – Jag alskar dig
Swiss-German – Ich lieb Di
Surinam – Mi lobi joe
Tagalog – Mahal kita
Taiwanese – Wa ga ei li
Tahitian – Ua Here Vau Ia Oe
Tamil – Nan unnai kathalikaraen
Telugu – Nenu ninnu premistunnanu
Thai – Chan rak khun (to male)
Thai – Phom rak khun (to female)
Turkish – Seni Seviyorum
Ukrainian – Ya tebe kahayu
Urdu – mai aap say pyaar karta hoo
Vietnamese – Anh ye^u em (to female)
Vietnamese – Em ye^u anh (to male)
Welsh – 'Rwy'n dy garu di
Yiddish – Ikh hob dikh
Yoruba – mo fe ran e

22.   Give Appreciation

The greatest gift in life is to be appreciative for all that we are and for those with whom we share our lives every day: as a parent, the ability to spend precious time in loving and nurturing a bond with the children; as entrepreneurs or business owners, the value of financial success and an invaluable network of team members to help run the show; as a worker, the daily interactions with various people in the work environment permits one to learn and be inspired, as a child in most Western and some Asian countries, the opportunity to be educated, playful and laugh with many other children in the school grounds.

All are great reasons as to why we should be thankful for how we live, what we have and who we associate with on a daily basis: to appreciate and feel blessed by every moment of life we are given, and to experience life fully with love, gratitude, enthusiasm and inner happiness. Show yourself to be a grateful person by enjoying, loving and living your life to the best of your abilities, in appreciation of yourself and others.

You can give love simply by showing your appreciation for the people who support and encourage you to be your best. If someone has had a positive impact on your life, then make sure that you acknowledge and appreciate it, either verbally or in a thank-you note. Whether it is financial, emotional or spiritual help, it is important that you let the person know that their kindness made a difference in your life.

Give others your time and let them know how much you love and appreciate them, especially when you know they are not going to be alive for long. Going for a nature walk or basking in the warm sun on winter afternoons with your grandparents or loving elders. Give kind and beautiful words to them such as 'I love every minute of the time that we are able to spend together, and thank you for teaching me from your life's wisdom'. This demonstrates your love and appreciation, you value them and feel that every precious moment you have with them is memorable and to be cherished.

Where ever the opportunity arises for you to say 'Thank you' in the presence of others is always an appreciation of goodwill. Give your appreciation when a stranger surprisingly helps you with your groceries to the car or opens a door for you. Sending a card with a thank-you message to an acquaintance, or someone you have just met who has invited you over to their place for chat or dinner; that is, if you have not yet verbally demonstrated your appreciation towards them. It is always a polite gesture to show how much you care about their kindness for inviting you to their home, meeting their family and in getting to know them as friends.

Writing thank -you letters are a long lost tradition that the next generation should try to revive! They do not necessarily need to be mailed out or handwritten, although it would be a nice touch. Most people communicate online daily and it only takes a quick second to type up a thank-you message to let somebody know they are appreciated.

I am sure that every day in your life presents many opportunities to give thanks to someone, or many people and circumstances where you experience gratitude. Being grateful is a measure of honouring your inner love, to see it in the kindness and love of others in return. In some ways, giving gratitude generally will bring an inflow of good karmic forces your way and abundance into your life.

Simply saying thank you and acknowledging the gratitude for others is all it takes!

Also, by creating positively impact gratitude aspirations and of moments that can be collectively recorded in our daily gratitude dairy or within in our thoughts. Helps us to be reminded of all the littlest things we can always be grateful for and are a blessing of gifts in our everyday life. Feel free to write down or speak of what you are grateful for.

So many people work hard day after day without feeling that they are having an impact on the world around them. If you let them know that their role in society is appreciated then it feels more worthwhile for them to continue their efforts. It is the same logic behind the need for give and take, mutually beneficial relationships. If someone is always extending their hand to help others but those people do not take the time to say thank you, then the relationship becomes unbalanced.

Although people do not do nice things with the expectation that their gesture will be appreciated, it is something that they should be able to count on. Think about the last time you opened a door for someone. Did they say thank you? Most people naturally say thank you when a stranger does something kind on their behalf, but they may forget to say it when the gesture comes from a parent or a close friend. We assume that our friends and family will be there to help us, so we do not always remember to show our gratitude.

The closer the relationship, the more important it is that you show appreciation. Giving appreciation is a free, easy and effective way for you to give your love. By sharing your gratitude to the other person, you are showing them that you love the role that they play in your life and the positive influence that they have on the world around them. If you do not appreciate what you have, it may not be there the next time that you need it.

Giving appreciation to others is respectful and shows you are good mannered and a thoughtful and polite person. Unfortunately, today, many younger people display little of these traits. Just observe the reality of this when you next commute on public transport by train or bus, or are in public spaces and shopping centres.

I question where this ignorance of how to treat other human beings will lead, if the younger generation does not commonly know how to demonstrate the meaning of love and kindness?! The absence of gratitude in people's lives and selfish attitudes are no excuse to not try to change, learn and grow as an appreciative and better person, in order to create a better world to live in. Circulating love by giving gratitude and respect to everyone you come across on a daily basis increases your chance to give back to others and the world.

23.   Share Successes

If something wonderful has happened to you, then you should feel proud and confident enough to share it with the people in your life who truly matter. If they love you then they will be excited by your accomplishment and want to share in the joy of your success. By you passing along the news of your good fortune, you may also inspire someone to step out of their own comfort zone to seek their own good fortune.

Reward and celebrate your successes with the people that matter most in your life. Create and host a big party or dinner to commemorate your successes and achievements. Celebrate your event at a funky joint or lavish restaurant that you have always wanted to go to, but have not had any great reasons to before. Now, you deserve it! Sharing love and happiness allows everyone to feel they are part of your life and supporting you along the way with your successes. Giving thanks to them is your real intention in holding the celebration.

Your achievement of success is a way to give back and show your appreciation to the ones that you love by rewarding yourself first, with the company of your loving and supporting family and friends in celebration. Treat yourself and your family members to a big holiday or that dream house or car that you have always wanted! Why not celebrate your success in your dream house?! After all, you deserve to achieve every goal that you have worked so hard for!

Celebrate your success by giving yourself the time to do what you have always loved and wanted to do. For myself, this is to go on a child-sponsoring charity trip to third world countries with Compassion, World Vision or a similar non-profit organisation. This is very rewarding for me, in knowing that I can help wherever I can to improve the many lives of underprivileged children. It is a starting point towards reaching my ultimate life goal of becoming an abundant philanthropist through my businesses and personal charity in the future.

Do not be timid or afraid to give people the reasons why you are celebrating your successes with them and displaying your wealth. They can only embrace their love and happiness for you in return, seeing that you have achieved so much in life and you are deserving of it as a complete confident, successful person. The REAL and improved YOU! You never know, other people probably are very inspired by your successes to make their own great changes and may want to follow in your footsteps to do the same. So be proud of yourself and your successes and be an inspiration!

Although, success should not change who you truly are as a loving, giving and appreciative person. I have heard and seen people who have undoubtedly changed for the worse when they have achieve successes. The person may have changed so much to the point that they do not know who they were in the first place and destroy their life and that of others around them.

> *Success in the right hands of the right person can do greatness and for the world. Contrary, success can deplete with obstinate corruption to many in the wrong hands of the wrong person. — Natasha Dao*

You should also share in the success of the people in your life. If someone has done something they are excited to share; then make sure to sincerely involve yourself in the conversation. Ask them questions about the experience, encourage them to describe it in detail and compliment them on their achievement. They will appreciate the recognition and they may inspire you in the process.

There are so many unfortunate, negative moments in our lives that we would prefer to forget. Tragedy, failure, abuse and destruction are unfortunate elements within everyone's life, which is why it is so vital that we celebrate every single good moment that comes our way. Anytime something wonderful has happened to you or someone else that you love, it is important that you shout it from the rooftops!

Be excited, feel excited and share your successes with the rest of the world!

You should also share the perks and financial rewards that come with your successes. There is no fun having wealth if you cannot really enjoy it by spending it on the people you love. Use a portion of any financial successes to reward your inner self and to help gratify your happiness and appreciation of your successes, such as to give back to worthwhile charities or causes. The successful sale of this book I am more than happy, knowingly that a proportion of sales is assigned to my nominated charities of Compassion, Caritas and World Vision. And I thank you for your support in purchasing this book. ☺

Share your rewards confidently with your loved ones in happy celebrations, parties and gatherings. Give gifts to your family, children and friends of things that they have always desired. Realistically, the rewards of your hard work will feel even more incredible when you have the pleasure of enjoying them with others.

The only wealth which you will keep forever is the wealth you are happily to share.

There is nothing more than having that special someone to share the enjoyment of your life's journey and rounds of successes with you. Celebrating all the love and support the other person (possibly your partner or your spouse) has generously provided you is important. They have been with you through the rough and challenging times, and they continue to cheer you on and provide you with the unconditional love and support that helped you to achieve your goals. It is very worthwhile having your partner share and celebrate your successes with.

Great success could be something work related or it could come from reaching a personal goal, but most often it is the result of hard work and dedication. It is not something that instantly happens without effort, which is why it is so important that you celebrate it. You put in the time, effort and commitment to successfully achieve your goal and that is why you deserve to enjoy the benefits of your hard work. You earned it!

24. Set Big Goals for Yourself!

To expand your potential, you need to continuously learn, grow and go beyond your everyday comfort zone. Discover your uniqueness and creativity as a special individual. Everyone is unique, we all have special gifts — our skills, talents and creativity.

You are never limited when you strive to be a whole person and work to achieve your highest potential as a person. I believe every human is here to thrive and not to just be complacent and live an ordinary life, just working to survive. That is not what truly defines being human. Build up a sense of contentment, of gratitude, self-love and confidence, and pursue growing to become a better person every day.

Give yourself a reason to dream big and set high goals in your life. If you do not, you are only selling yourself short by not allowing your fullest capabilities and potential self to shine. Create the life that you deserve to live!

Learning to love and believe in yourself should inspire you to set bigger goals for your life. By challenging yourself, you will find your true potential in life. There is so much that you can do in life, if you set your mind to it. Like Napoleon Hill says: 'Your thoughts will become things'. Live inspiringly by activating your dreams, stretching beyond your desires by holding firmly to self-love and belief. Do not let anyone tell you that your dream is too big or unrealistic. It is really your mind that will limit your dream life eventuating.

I dream my painting and then I paint my dream. — Van Gough

People often discount their ability to pursue any goal that they feel is too big or out of their reach. However, it is only fear that makes them afraid to act on their goals and big dream. I think it is great if your big dream makes you feel incredibly scared, but yet terrifyingly exciting at the same time! Just do not be overwhelmed by your fear of challenges, so that you become paralysed or procrastinate. By tackling the challenges, you will make many adventurous, challenging and fun discoveries and you will find out more about yourself as you progress towards your goals and big dream.

Life is a journey of continuous growth and self-discovery. You can learn something new about yourself every day, either impactful or not. You can improve yourself by asking simple questions such as 'Why did it happen?' and 'How does this affect me?' and 'What have I learnt from this?' List the many reasons and answers to these questions on paper, or in your head, if you do not have access to a pen and paper. This will help you to clarify and define your choices and options towards making better decisions.

Understanding how you can improve yourself is a learning process, and creates robust building blocks to a higher self-confidence and an internal growth of self-love. Not everything in your life will proceed with certainties and one hundred per cent success. Be open to the various changes and be flexible along the journey towards meeting your goals. It is the uncertainties, trials and tribulations that will help you to find your better self. Life's many challenges will teach and encourage you to step up to take bigger actions. You have to remember, this is part and parcel of stepping beyond your comfort zone, courageously staring fear in the face and working towards your dream.

Life is meant to be experienced and you should not pass up opportunities simply because you are afraid of failing. You deserve to achieve everything that you have ever dreamt about, and the only way you can do it is by setting goals and sticking to them.

Spread your wings and fly!

One great way to set a goal and stick to it is by verbalising it to the people who you respect. By sharing your goal with the people in your life, you will most likely receive their encouragement and help to reach it. Also, by saying it out loud, you are confirming your commitment and allowing others to hold you accountable. Sometimes it is easier to back down from a challenge when no one knows you have been challenged. When people know what you are trying to do, they will help motivate you to stay on the path to success.

Strong self-belief and positive gratitude affirmations every day are great enforcers, helping you to stay grounded and stick to your goals and dreams, keeping you fully inspired and on your target daily. Having a plan of action and workbook of your daily goals can immensely help you to keep focus and on track of your bigger goals and dream: http://tinyurl.com/nd3unss.

Your big dream is the ultimate future vision you have of your life. Having an end in mind as to where you want to go in life and a vision of your goals and achievements helps to pave your way to achieve success. Although, remember that life is about the journey and experiences, and not only the destination.

The reward of accolades and successes as you reach stepping stones to your goals, generates motivation and personal positive inspiration, and moves you closer to being able to 'taste and touch' your big dream! Celebrate every success with personal rewards or gifts for yourself or celebrate with your friends, partner and loved ones.

> *Faith, is the ability to see the invisible and believe in the incredible and that is what enables believers to receive what the masses think is impossible.*
> — *Clarence Smithison*

Setting and reaching goals will build your confidence and inspire you to do more with your life. When you realise that you can do something that you always thought you couldn't, it reminds you that the possibilities are endless. You will experience a greater feeling of self-worth and you will be inspired to set even bigger goals.

Setting goals is the gateway to success. If you settle with what you already have in life, then you cannot expect new successes will just fall into your lap. You need to create new challenges for yourself and push yourself to see how great your life can be. You never know what you can accomplish until you try!

25.   Care for the Environment

How you live, breathe and even eat will affect the world and the environment on a large scale. I feel we are ALL responsible for loving and caring for any neglect or damaged we have inflicted on mother earth. There is still time to change your attitudes and behaviours towards loving and nurturing the environment for a happier and cleaner world for everyone to live in.

You can reduce everyday carbon emissions, and helping to achieve a cleaner airspace is by getting into the habit of recycling all of your waste products such as plastics, papers and many household packaged goods. Just look for the recycling 'repeat' triangle symbol on the back of every package. This indicates the package is appropriate for recycling. This symbol is relevant in Australia, so you probably need to see what is applicable in your country. I am sure there are plenty of these products that you can and should recycle to help the environment. In return, you will also help to minimise the insurmountable landfills that we are breathing in every day. Start today, recycle and repeat!

Be grateful for the goodness, wildlife and natural beauty of the environment that surrounds you. Be thankful for mother earth's magnificent creation in which we can all co-exist and co-create, to live in harmony and enjoyment. Take pride in and respect and be responsible for how you treat, love and care for the environment.

Dispose of your rubbish in the bin appropriately in public areas and at shopping centres. Do not wait for others such as cleaners to pick up your rubbish for you. Always pick up after yourself, because you care and are responsible for your own actions and behaviours.

Don't you just dislike seeing people disposing rubbish freely over their shoulders, as though they do not care less about their actions, let alone caring for the environment! I have to admit, this really annoys me and it is not good to see. I will always pick up rubbish when I see that this needs to be done, not because I feel that I am responsible for other people's ignorance and lack of care , but because I care and feel responsible for the environment.

Remember to always pick up rubbish, even if it is not of your own. If you happen to walk by and see a piece of rubbish on the footpath or along your way, give your time to care and dispose of that rubbish in a nearby bin. Set a good example for young children and encourage them to adopt this good behaviour in loving and caring for the environment and for the future. We can all learn from one another by helping each other to take responsibility for our own actions towards the environment, so we can all live and breathe in a better, healthier and cleaner world.

Water is another precious commodity that supports human needs and all living things. Without water, nothing will survive, all the animal, wildlife and plants. The human body can only survive forty-eight hours or so without water, before it shuts down from dehydration. The global water surface is evaporating rapidly, due to a world depletion of natural resources, less rain and more droughts. All of which, it is claimed, are the cause of the current destruction of the ozone layer.

Therefore, it is very important to use and save water wisely wherever you can! When you shower, turn off the water tap while you are shampooing and scrubbing yourself. You will be amazed at how many litres of water you will save when you do this! And, of course, try to minimise your shower time, which will lessen your water usage. I know you probably have heard this before, but it is worth a reminder to always turn off the tap when brushing your teeth or cleansing your face. Do not allow the water to run unnecessarily in the background. As a matter of fact, apply this wherever possible at home.

You can save water by consuming it smartly and conservatively in the bathroom, kitchen, laundry, outdoors and driveway and in the garden. Make every effort to change how you use water and help to make a difference to the environment. Live to save and conserve water now!

In the same manner that it is important for you to care for your body, it is also important that you take proper care of the environment that you live in. Our earth is a blessing and we need to preserve it so that future generations can enjoy it. You will find by doing your part to help the environment, you will receive the personal satisfaction of knowing that you had a positive impact on something as crucial as the world!

When people become focused solely on their own lives, they neglect to do their basic duty in caring for the world around them. The basic part that everyone is capable of doing every day is the three 'Rs': recycle, reduce and reuse. Grade school children are taught its importance, yet many adults still neglect to make the effort. It does not take much effort on your part, yet it has such a critical impact on the environment.

It is important that you respect the earth and that you try to do your part to improve it. You can plant a tree, pick up litter at local parks, or help by donating spare change to environmental causes. It is the little things that have the greatest impact.

I once volunteered to help clean a local stream of garbage and the experience was incredible. I could see the change I made, plus I met several like-minded people as we combined our efforts to restore a beautiful stream to its intended condition.

We only have one world, so it is important that you do your part to take care of it!

26.   Be Grateful!

Being alive, healthy and able to enjoy your life is a gift that not everyone gets to experience. So many people are born into countries where health and freedom are hard for the average person to obtain. They are grateful simply to have clean drinking water, a loaf of bread or a warm blanket on a chilly night.

Do you ever feel lucky that you have a glass of water to drink?

We should not only feel blessed for all the major things that are given to us, but also the little things that we tend to take for granted. Appreciate the fact that you have food, shelter and good health. We also need to be grateful for the people who care about us and the people who are there to make our life more enjoyable.

'Gratitude is not only the greatest of virtues, but the parent of all the others.'
— Cicero

You should also take time to appreciate the beautiful world that surrounds you. Even if you do not live near majestic mountains, a beautiful beach or a natural forest, there is still incredible scenery all around you every day. You should take the time to appreciate your neighbour's flowerbed, enjoy a sunny day or even delight in the sight of children laughing or playing at a local park. Simply slow down and look around! There is beauty to be found everywhere and all you need to do is to make the time to really appreciate it.

Appreciate and be grateful for one another and each other's presence. Enjoy the company of others through many happy and friendly conversations. Share love and joy and be surrounded by your family, friends and acquaintances. Even create new friendships with strangers or new introductions. Give your time to be with others and share those moments together in gratitude. You never know, you might not get another opportunity to do so. Make your life, sociably alive and get out there and meet and greet!

Connect with your neighbours or even that lost lover or childhood friend. Facebook them or give them a call to show how much you appreciate and care for their love and support in your life. You value the relationship and the person that they are, and all the experiences that were shared. Give each other the chance to be lovingly appreciative for the time spent together in happy memories. Appreciate and value of all the people that have been part of your life.

As an appreciative token to your everyday life, you can simply give someone a personal gift such as a beautiful flower from the garden bed or a loving gesture. Give others gifts that need not be purchased that are inexpensive. The simple gestures in giving are essentially coming from your kind, caring and loving thoughts for others and your personal gratitude. When you give, you will feel a sense of self-gratification in loving and the inner joy of gratefulness. The key ingredient to living an abundant and fulfilled happy and loving life is to always be giving and in return is the notion of receiving. The complete full circle of appreciation and life.

Be grateful for people, places and life experiences. Every one of them is special in their own way. Too often people do not appreciate what they have until it is gone. Start each day by being grateful for the ability to get out of bed and then think about each step as you take it. Have a daily gratitude journal or think gratefully, detailing all that you are grateful for that day and count all your blessings! Think about the hot soapy water in your shower, your nice clean outfit, your warm breakfast and the reason that gets you up each morning. You are blessed with many comforts within minutes of starting your day. Most of us take these things for granted and do not realise that not everyone has the same luxuries.

Being truly grateful means appreciating everything that life has to offer you. Treasure the special moments that you share and do not miss out on potential gratitude moments. If you are healthy and able to enjoy life, take advantage of it. I truly believe that if everyone lived each and every day like it was their last this world would be a lot more loving, kinder, brighter, happier and more satisfying place.

The attitude of gratitude in every aspect of your life is responsible for the many grateful blessings you will encounter as a result. Some I would say are unspeakable moments of amazing miracles and experiences. You do not need to question or know how or when these 'miracles' take place, other than to be grateful for all you are and be fully awaken to enjoy every moment of these manifolds experiences. When this happens, just simply and humbly receive with a big 'Thank you!'

In every karmic aspect of life, what comes around will go around. You might experience a round of great gratitude encounters with the general public or with a shopping assistant when you acknowledge the good service that they have provided you with. Just say 'Thank you for your help.' You may find more surprises because of their consideration and willingness to help you further in finding something you are looking for, even though it is not their duty.

143

So, being grateful for your everyday circumstances and helping yourself to live a much more purposeful and enriching life will allow you to embrace inner truth and blissful happiness. Even in the worst of times, you can feel humble gratitude for learning and growing from within because of these unexpected problems. Giving gratitude to whatever that might arise in your life empowers you and helps overcome any difficulties with understanding, love and self-confidence to your highest ability.

Importantly, be grateful for your divine self and for the talents and skills that are given to you as a living and breathing and higher potential human being. You were born into this world with divine intervention to co-create with others, to do greatness with your God-given gifts. So make use of them wherever you can to serve and do greatness for others.

Making the most of the opportunities you are given is a great way to show your gratitude. If you are able to dance, then dance! If you are able to get in a good university, do not turn down the experience. If you are capable of greatness, then seek greatness. There are so many people out there who are deprived of the same blessings that you take for granted and, out of respect for them, you should never let your blessings go unused.

Appreciate what you have in life instead of focusing on what you feel may be lacking. If you stop and think about everything you have to be grateful for then you will quickly realise how lucky you really are. Say thank you to the people who make your life better, be grateful for all the wonderful opportunities that you have and appreciate your health, wealth and success no matter how fragile it may seem at the time. Be grateful for what you have and true happiness will follow.

KARMA

empowerment

GIVING **goodness** non-judgemental

mindful Appreciation

Caring GRATITUDE **growth**

gift loving & positive actions attitude

INSPIRATIONAL RESPECT

self-love *kindness* acceptance

CONSIDERATE self-will

Enhance your gratitude words by finding in the crossword.

Y	G	S	G	N	I	B	S	J	A
E	R	R	E	N	E	W	G	O	B
V	A	Z	A	V	I	N	O	U	U
I	T	R	I	T	I	V	D	L	N
E	E	L	E	S	I	G	O	O	D
C	F	W	S	H	F	T	W	L	A
E	U	E	G	V	T	M	U	Q	N
R	L	U	F	E	P	O	H	D	C
B	S	A	T	T	I	T	U	D	E
E	T	A	I	C	E	R	P	P	A

GRATITUDE, ATTITUDE, BLESSINGS, GRATEFUL, LOVING, GIVE, ABUNDANCE, NOW, APPRECIATE, RECEIVE, GOOD, HOPEFUL, SOUL, GOD, LIVE, OTHER, NEW, BRINGS,

27.   Give the Gift of Life

At the time of writing this book, I have not yet experienced the blessings of motherhood. But in due course, I will have the opportunity to do so and am looking forward to one day embracing a new gift of life that I can give to myself and my future husband. Seeing the experiences of my family members, relatives and friends as mothers has taught me what it means to miss out on the love and joy that I and a partner can create as our little gift of life. After all, I absolutely love and adore children and can foresee that I will one day have a family of my own.

The greatest gift of life is in the gift of love and life's miracles, given from above. — Natasha Dao

The loving unity of two people creating a baby and forming a beautiful family of their own is said to be the greatest gift or miracle that they can perform together selflessly. Sometimes, in many relationships, planning to bring a child into this world is unquestioned and may be disregarded for many selfish reasons. But when a child does enter into the world, not only the love in the relationship expands, but the deep lovingness as a whole family unit. In most cases, a child will lovingly unite and bond the two people and their struggling relationship to a higher level of oneness and togetherness.

I have seen this in many couples whose situation and lives have been transformed to become very loving with one another again and endearing parents. You can see the immense love that they show to one another and to their child is what they live for, their family happiness. Parents playing and running around with their children in the park, laughing and sharing their time together is a beautiful sight that brings sheer joy, love and happiness such as only a family can create.

I love witnessing these scenes, either in public with my family, relatives and friends. This, more than ever, gives me a reason to be excited about when I can have a family with my partner. Understanding the importance of having a family as part of your life, if you do not already, enhances the happiness and loving joy and completeness of your world when you give the gift of life.

There is nothing more precious than giving a new life into this world, to hold and love as of your own. To share the bundle of love with your family and friends is a blessing of joy in a very special gratitude moment, from the early stage of conception to the growing stages of nine months pregnancy.

It seems more and more couples are choosing not to give the world the most incredible gift there is to give. They are making the tough decision not to bring a child into the world due to finances, their career, their lifestyle or other deeply personal reasons. There is nothing wrong with deciding not to have a child. You should never feel forced to procreate, especially if that is something that you do not want out of your life.

However, you will be missing out on the most powerful gift you can give.

Although, it may not be necessary to have a child in order to find an abundance of happiness in your life, it is certainly one way that happiness is almost a guarantee. When you hold that helpless, innocent child in your arms and you feel the love radiating between you, you will realise why it is always referred to as the gift of life.

Choosing to have a baby and making sure that you raise the child in a supportive, nurturing, loving environment is a gift that will literally last a lifetime. Your love will be reflected in your child's affection and respect for you as their parent. When you are blessed to have a child, make sure that you give that child a life worth living. It does not take great financial means, but it does take tremendous love.

Notice the blessing in everything big and small. Dwell on the beauty in all I see, hear, touch, taste, smell. Realise that everything is a gift from the Almighty and is put there by God in order to enjoy and learn from.
— Dr. Benjamin Franklin

Children are a huge commitment and they require you to give of yourself daily without ever expecting anything in return. They need to be fed, taught, supported and loved until they are old enough and capable of caring for themselves. Even after they have left your home, your love and support doesn't go away.

Children look to their parents for guidance and support throughout their lives and the bond that is created is unshakeable. There will be rough moments, especially during the teenage years where it will feel like the love is gone, but it never really goes away. Even if they say they don't love you anymore, deep down you can have faith that the love will resurface.

The bond created between mother and child or between father and child is stronger than any other force and it will be resilient no matter how many times it is tested. Give the greatest gift of yourself by committing your life to another human being and the abundance of love you receive in return will be undeniable.

If you are not ready for a child or not sure that you want one, you can pick up a pet instead. There are so many loving kittens and puppies out there that are in desperate need of a good home. By taking care of a helpless animal, you are selflessly sharing your love. Most likely, your newfound furry friend will show you love in return, but regardless your love will have a positive impact on their life and your own.

There is no greater responsibility and commitment than having a child, closely followed by owning a pet. You are agreeing to care for and support a defenceless, helpless creature for life. It is amazing that one person would take on such a huge undertaking, but the love and life experiences that you will get in return are priceless.

28.   Conclusion

Have Faith

Happiness will come when you learn to have faith that things are meant to be and there is no point stressing over temporary problems.

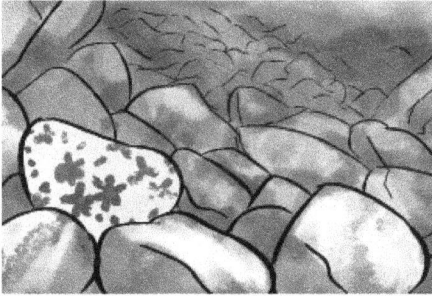

You can trust that everything will eventually work out, if you maintain a positive attitude and believe in yourself and have faith. If you live a good life, and do good for others, then it only makes sense that you will experience the same in return.

Things will eventually work out in your best interest, but sometimes you have to endure a few rough patches in order to truly appreciate the good times. Everything happens for a reason, it just may take a little while before you realise the reason behind a challenging part of your life. For example, I faced many challenges growing up, but if it was not for those difficult experiences, I wouldn't have the advice or guidance to give to you now.

Good things happen to good people, so it is important that you continue to have faith and not cause additional friction when times are tough. Other people may treat you poorly, but that is no excuse for treating someone else the same way. Things will get easier and you can rely on the fact that you won't be given anything to deal with that you can't handle.

Be Happy!

The most important thing is that you make choices in life that are going to make you truly happy. You deserve to be happy and there is no reason why you should not spend some of your time and energy on securing your own happiness. When you are reaching out to the world and all of the people who matter in your life, you may sometimes forget to take care of yourself! You also matter!

Happiness in life comes from appreciating everything you have, surrounding yourself with positive people and feeling good about yourself. Many of the virtues and advice expressed in this book will naturally lead you to greater happiness.

> *What we call the secret of happiness is no more a secret than our willingness to choose life. — Leo Buscaglia*

Life is short and it should be lived to the fullest. You should chase your dream and set high goals, and then reward yourself when you have accomplished something special. I truly realised that happiness is a choice. You can allow your life to drag you down or you can decide to be happy and look for the good in every situation. Not everything in life is necessarily fun, but you can make the most out of it instead of dwelling on the negative. Focus on the happy moments and it will make the sad moments more bearable.

> *Your life is the sum result of all the choices you make, both consciously and unconsciously. If you can control the process of choosing, you can take control of all aspects of your life. You can find the freedom that comes from being in charge of yourself. — Robert F. Bennett.*

There is something wonderful that happens within when you realise that you have control over your own life. You have the ability to forgive the past, appreciate the present and prepare for your future. You can decide to make it as happy as possible by surrounding yourself with love and gratitude or you can give in to your weaknesses. Once you realise that it is in your hands, I hope you will choose to live up to your strengths and be happy living a fulfilling of a higher purpose life!

Love Life!

One of the simplest ways for you to find happiness is by choosing to love the life that you are given. Appreciate your blessings, treasure your friends and enjoy each day. Look at everything that you have instead of what you might feel is lacking in your life. When you are happy with your own life, you will be more ready to receive love and open to experiencing everything life has to offer and of greater success.

You can find real love and happiness simply by how you choose to fill your days. By spending time with your family and friends, doing things that you enjoy together and helping spread a positive attitude, it will result in a greater love of life itself. You can find love in your own life simply by connecting with other people in a meaningful way. What could be easier than that?

Life is short and it is so important that you do the things that make you happy. It is even better if you can use your talents to spread love. If you love painting, then paint someone a beautiful portrait! If you love running, sign up for a charity run! If you enjoy nature walks, go and surround yourself in that environment, or even do a bushwalk!

Do what is necessary to fulfil your life in full colours, and importantly do what you absolutely love and do it as often as possible.

Spread a little love and you will feel so much more in return!

So many of the old clichés we hear in life are actually true and I am sure many of them crossed your mind while you were reading this book.

Everything happens for a reason!

You will get out of life what you put in it!

Good things happen to good people!

The reasons those clichés have lasted the test of time is because they have been proven over and over again.

This book alone has countless examples of how everything really does happen for a reason. Our hardships are life lessons and the good times are meant to be appreciation and inspiration. No matter how bleak things may seem at times, things eventually work themselves out.

You have to bear through the storm to see the silver lining that waits at the end of the rainbow. — Natasha Dao.

You will get out of life what you put in it. If you work hard, you will be rewarded financially, physically or emotionally. If you give of yourself to the better of the world, you will feel wonderfully amazed about yourself and the world around you.

It is also true that good things happen to good people. If you are a good person who does good things for other people, the odds are that people will notice and they will be there for you when you need it. If you maintain a positive attitude and look for the good in the world, you will most likely find it. It is so simple to find an abundance of happiness in your life and you will start seeing it everywhere once you make the choice to be happy.

> *'I've learned that no matter what happens, or how bad it seems today, life does go on, and it will be better tomorrow.'*
>
> *'I've learned that regardless of your relationship with your parents, you'll miss them when they're gone from your life.'*
>
> *'I've learned that you shouldn't go through life with a catcher's mitt on both hands; you need to be able to throw things back.'*
>
> *'I've learned that whenever I decide something with an open heart, I usually make the right decision.'*
>
> *'I've learned that even when I have pains, I don't have to be one.'*
>
> *'I've learned that every day you should reach out and touch someone. People love a warm hug, or just a friendly pat on the back.'*
>
> *'I've learned that I still have a lot to learn.'*
>
> *— Maya Angelou*

I want to be able to empower you and show you why and how it is important to appreciate every aspect of life, including the little things, to help people who are truly in need and to treasure the time that you spend with other people. In activating your inner love and gratitude, you will subsequently discover your higher purpose of life. By freely giving and sharing your love with the world, the world will love you in return. Happiness comes naturally to people who know they are loved.

To continue spreading the love and gratitude of happiness, take this message and pass it on to the people in your life. Share the wisdom you have gained from my stories, teachings and knowledge, and inspire others to discover their higher purpose calling to find happiness in their own life. The more you can create positive change, the better you will feel about your contribution to the world. Life and love are meant to be given, and these gifts can have an incredible impact when you choose to share them.

> *Embrace life in constant Giving and Sharing Love and Gratitude onto others, enhancing our lives to be abundantly fulfilled with great happiness of inner peace and Compassion – creating a better world for all humanity. — Natasha Dao*

Wishing you a lifetime of giving and sharing love!

Quotes Page References

Giving connects two people, the giver and the receiver, and this connection gives birth to a new sense of belonging.
— Deepak Chopra. (Page 21)

CHAPTER FIVE

Giving gives a new form of life and real meaning to the gift of generosity and in receiving – the ebb and flow of continuous abundance. — Natasha Dao. (Page 36)

You do not have to be rich to be generous. If he has the spirit of true generosity, a pauper can give like a prince.
— Corrine V. Wells. (Page 37)

Without Love, life fades and dies. Where as with Love, life flourishes and is lived. — Natasha Dao. (Page 39)

To get you must Give. I've scarce enough bread, and of course one must live; but I would partake of life's bountiful store....Then you must Give more. As he gave of himself in useful living, then joy crowned his days, for he grew rich in Giving. — Arthur William Beer. (Page 40)

Be generous, be giving, behold the gift to know the meaning of receiving. The total act of inner appreciation. — Natasha Dao. (Page 41)

CHAPTER SIX

'Be the best and wholesome person you can and as onto others.'

'Live life to the fullest and don't take anything for granted, by LOVING life with ultimate COMPASSION.'

'Embrace; love; life and celebrate!'

— Natasha Dao. (Page 43)

Optimism is the epitome mindset to grow and expand personally as to live for a brighter, fulfilled future. — Natasha Dao. (Page 45)

Change your thoughts. Change your life. — Dr Wayne Dyer. (Page 49)

CHAPTER SEVEN

Love within from the heart, embellishes such great joy and happiness where only one can feel deeply remotely natural to give with all to another.
— Natasha Dao. (Page 51)

Love with without prejudice, give the virtue of continuous acceptance to everyone and to yourself, no less than to others to love freely. For love is endless, provokingly generous to give by many and absolutely everyone infectiously worldwide. — Natasha Dao (Page 52)

The wheel of life keeps turning so what you give or take will eventually come back to you. Make sure you look forward to it's arrival.
— Sally Eichhorst. (Page 53)

CHAPTER EIGHT

Love everything and everyone; Release all judgement and resistance; Allow yourself to just be joyful...regardless of what happens.
— Harrison Klein. (Page 57)

Laughter gives us distance. It allows us to step back from an event, deal with it and then move on. — Bob Newhart. (Page 57)

CHAPTER NINE

Only the development of COMPASSION and understanding for others can bring us the tranquillity and HAPPINESS we all seek.
— Dalai Lama. (Page 64)

CHAPTER TEN

Wisdom is not a product of schooling but of the lifelong attempt to acquire it.
— Albert Einstein. (Page 67)

Hindsight is helpful and foresight is a blessing but insight makes wise men wise. — Garry Mac. (Page 68)

Anyone who stops learning is old, whether at twenty or eighty. Anyone who keeps learning stays young. The greatest thing in life is to keep your mind young. — Henry Ford. (Page 69)

CHAPTER ELEVEN

The best portion of a good man's life – his little, nameless, un-remembered acts of KINDNESS & LOVE. — William Wordsworth. (Page 73)

*If you can't feed a hundred people, then feed just one.
— Mother Teresa. (Page 75)*

CHAPTER TWELVE

To forgive is the highest, most beautiful form of love. In return, you will receive untold peace and happiness. — Robert Muller. (Page 81)

CHAPTER FOURTEEN

If your actions inspire others to dream more, learn more, do more and become more, you are a leader. — John Quincy Adams. (Page 91)

CHAPTER FIFTEEN

*When you are sharing your time, love and gratitude in special moments with others, you are creating a living moment of real-time happiness.
— Natasha Dao. (Page 93)*

Gratitude for the present moment and the fullness of life now is the true prosperity. — Eckhart Tolle. (Page 94)

*When we give cheerfully and accept gratefully, everyone is blessed.
— Maya Angelou. (Page 95)*

CHAPTER SIXTEEN

*The weak can never forgive. Forgiveness is the attribute of the strong.
— Mahatma Gandhi. (Page 97)*

Forgiveness is more than just a verbal response when someone apologises. It has to be felt within and come from a place of peace and acceptance. Everyone has done something wrong at one point or another during the course of their life and, although it does not excuse their behaviour, they are only human. They can easily fall victim to temptation or evil without realising the pain their actions are causing. Forgiving others is in the healing of forgiving oneself. — Natasha Dao. (Page 99)

CHAPTER SEVENTEEN

Seek seldom in others, helping and nurturing our love and support for one kind. — Natasha Dao. (Page 103)

CHAPTER EIGHTEEN

Treat others as you would have done unto yourself.
— Natasha Dao. (Page 105)

CHAPTER NINETEEN

Breathe. Let go. And remind yourself that this very moment is the only one you know you have for sure. — Oprah Winfrey. (Page 110)

LOVE is the only reality and it is not a mere sentiment. It is the ultimate truth that lies at the HEART of CREATION.
— Rabindranath Tagore. (Page 111)

CHAPTER TWENTY-ONE

The more you are motivated by LOVE, the more fearless and free your action will be. — Dalai Lama. (Page 119)

Always tell someone how you feel because opportunities are lost in the blink of any eye, but regret can last forever. — Unknown. (Page 121)

CHAPTER TWENTY-THREE

Success in the right hands of the right person can do greatness and for the world. Contrary, success can deplete with obstinate corruption to many in the wrong hands of the wrong person.
— Natasha Dao. (Page 130)

CHAPTER TWENTY-FOUR

I dream my painting and then I paint my dream. — Van Gough. (Page 133)

Faith, is the ability to see the invisible and believe in the incredible and that is what enables believers to receive what the masses think is impossible.
— Clarence Smithison. (Page 136)

CHAPTER TWENTY-SIX

Gratitude is not only the greatest of virtues, but the parent of all the others.
— Cicero. (Page 141)

CHAPTER TWENTY-SEVEN

The greatest gift of life is in the gift of love and life's miracles, given from above. — Natasha Dao. (Page 147)

Notice the blessing in everything big and small. Dwell on the beauty in all I see, hear, touch, taste, smell. Realise that everything is a gift from the Almighty and is put there by God in order to enjoy and learn from.
— Dr. Benjamin Franklin. (Page 149)

CHAPTER TWENTY-EIGHT

What we call the secret of happiness is no more a secret than our willingness to choose life. — Leo Buscaglia. (Page 152)

Your life is the sum result of all the choices you make, both consciously and unconsciously. If you can control the process of choosing, you can take control of all aspects of your life. You can find the freedom that comes from being in charge of yourself. — Robert F. Bennett. (Page 152)

You have to bear through the storm to see the silver lining that awaits at the end of the rainbow. — Natasha Dao. (Page 154)

'I've learned that no matter what happens, or how bad it seems today, life does go on, and it will be better tomorrow.'

'I've learned that regardless of your relationship with your parents, you'll miss them when they're gone from your life.'

'I've learned that you shouldn't go through life with a catcher's mitt on both hands; you need to be able to throw things back.'

'I've learned that whenever I decide something with an open heart, I usually make the right decision.'

'I've learned that even when I have pains, I don't have to be one.'

164

'I've learned that every day you should reach out and touch someone. People love a warm hug, or just a friendly pat on the back.'

'I've learned that I still have a lot to learn.'

— *Maya Angelou. (Page 155)*

Embrace life in constant Giving and Sharing Love and Gratitude onto others, enhancing our lives to be abundantly fulfilled with great happiness of inner peace and Compassion – creating a better world for all humanity.
— *Natasha Dao. (Page 156)*

A Biography of

Natasha Dao

"How could humanity of such children in poverty is unserved with no human compassion and love"? This was the question Natasha Dao has consciously raised in her mind since the day she had revisited her motherland country in Vietnam. As a refugee migrating to Australia at a very young age of four with her mother and grandma amongst seven of her other younger children. Sixteen years later when revisiting her home country origin at an isolated village of Ba Ria on the South Eastern part of Vietnam.

She was deeply heart broken and emotionally moved from what she had seen in the staggering numbers of homeless and underprivileged children, daily struggling to survive on the streets in extremely destitute conditions, for some were in neglected orphanages. Natasha could strongly empathize of how the children must be feeling of being so unloved and unwanted, letting alone of not having the necessities to live. At the age seven, she was a sexual and violent victim of being unloved and unwanted with little hope of her future ahead. Through a lot of pain, resentment, anger and unknowingly of what love was, she grew up tiresomely trying to find love within her family, her partner relationship and with her friends.

Through her personal and past experiences as of today, at age 37 she is a person of immeasurable generosity with immense love and compassion for people, especially in supporting for underprivileged and misfortunate children around third world countries. Natasha's philanthropic works currently involves in writing her upcoming best-seller book of "LOVE & GRATITUDE". The book publication will provide the readers of self-empowerment and in the transformation of finding their higher purpose to their awakening path of life. All in the activation of healing with inner Love & Gratitude to all aspect of life. In overall perspective, the book is the tool for generating great compassion and happiness within ourselves and our surroundings, effectively creating a global wave of love onto others, making a lasting positive change. A proportion of all proceeds from the sales of this book will be generously supporting well serving charities for Compassion, Caritas and World Vision.

Natasha other philanthropic works also includes I Am Love Campaign https://www.facebook.com/natasha.dao.3 and http://lovinggratitude.com. In sharing a passion for service for a happier, healthier humanity, changing the lives of children in poverty around under-developing countries. In every aspect, her desired objective is to induce a world conscious of unity, love, peace and harmony for all human kind. A generous proportion of proceeds of sales in merchandises and books will also be in supporting the above charities.

In the past and of presently, Natasha have generously supported with many donations and volunteered works with Children Starlight Foundation, Compassion and Caritas, Breast Cancer, Multiple Sclerosis, Homeless People, and Foodbank for Flood Victims with many donations and voluntary services.

Personally, Natasha Dao enjoys meditation, yoga and have a love of life for nature, animals, children, people, art, reading and writing and business.

www.ingramcontent.com/pod-product-compliance
Lightning Source LLC
Chambersburg PA
CBHW032100080426
42733CB00006B/353